The Russian Navy:
Myth and Reality

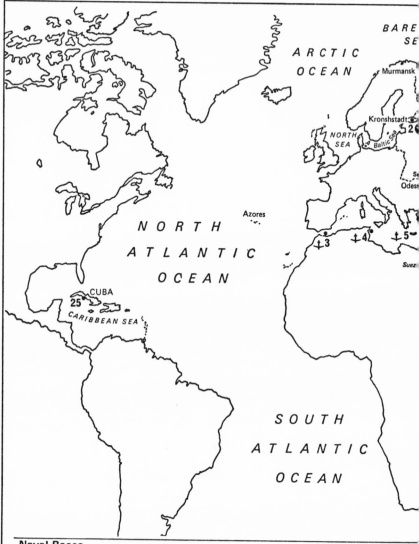

ARCTIC OCEAN

BARE
SE

Murmansk

Kronshstadt

NORTH
SEA

Baltic Sea

2

Odess

Azores

NORTH

ATLANTIC

OCEAN

3

4

5

Suez

CUBA

25

CARIBBEAN SEA

SOUTH

ATLANTIC

OCEAN

Naval Bases

1 Kola Inlet, Murmansk HQ and main naval base for the Soviet Northern Fleet: 160 submarines and 56 major surface warships

2 Baltic Fleet based on Kronshtadt and HQ at Baltiysk: 12 submarines and 47 major surface warships

8 Crimea base complex: Odessa, Nikolayev, Sevastopol. Black Sea Fleet (including Caspian Flotilla and Mediterranean Squadron): 19 submarines and 59 major surface warships

NB All estimated strengths are approximate

⭐ *Main naval bases*

20 Soviet Pacific Fleet HQ at Vladivostok: 74 submarines and 57 major surface warships

21 Sovetskaya Gavan

22 Petropavlovsk

Naval base facilities

7 One-time Soviet naval base facilities at Alexandria and Port Said

14 Mogadiscio (Somali Republic)

15 Berbera (Somali Republic)

16 Mauritius: Aeroflot flies in relief crews for Soviet trawlers

OVIET UNION

CASPIAN
SEA

SEA

Petropavlovsk •22

23
24 •
•21 Sovetskaya
Gavan

Vladivostok
★ 20 SEA
OF JAPAN

PACIFIC

OCEAN

ARABIAN
SEA

17

15

14

•19

18
Andaman Is.

Maldive Is.
↓12

Seychelles
↓10

↓ 11 Chagos
Archipelago

INDIAN OCEAN

Mauritius
• •16

17 Aden: repair facilities

18 Port Blair, Andaman Islands: Indian
   naval base used by Soviet Fleet

19 Vishakhapatnam

25 Cienfuegos

9 Indian Ocean Anchorage 250 miles east
  of Durban

10 Seychelles

11 Chagos Archipelago

12 Maldive Islands

13 Soviet tankers refuel warships at anchor
   in the Mozambique channel

Anchorages ↓

3 Melilla Point/Alboran Island

4 Gulf of Hammamet ⎫
5 Crete   ⎬ Anchorage for
6 East of Cyprus ⎭ Mediterranean
                     Squadron

23 Komsomolsk ⎫
24 Khabarovsk ⎬ Shipbuilding yards

By the same Author

BLOCKADE: BERLIN AND THE COLD WAR

The Russian Navy: Myth and Reality

ERIC MORRIS

*Senior Lecturer, Department of War Studies
and International Affairs,
Royal Military Academy, Sandhurst*

STEIN AND DAY/*Publishers*/New York

First published in the United States 1977
Copyright © 1977 by Eric Morris
All rights reserved
Printed in the United States of America
Stein and Day /*Publishers*/Scarborough House,
Briarcliff Manor, N.Y. 10510

Library of Congress Cataloging in Publication Data

Morris, Eric, 1940-
    The Russian Navy.

    Bibliography p. 145
    Includes index.
    1. Russia (1923-   U.S.S.R.).   Voenno-Morskoi Flot.
2. Russia—Military policy.   I. Title.
VA573.M67   359.3′0947   77-7122
ISBN 0-8128-2324-9

To Pamela, Christopher
and Leah

Acknowledgements

In the writing of this book I owe a personal debt of gratitude to many people: to Michael McGwire, Professor of Military and Strategic Studies at Dalhousie University, Halifax, Nova Scotia; to the Naval Liaison Officers at Sandhurst, especially Lt. Cdr. Gaythorne Gough and his successor Lt. Cdr. Martin Knapp; to the experts in Soviet Studies, Brian Jones, Peter Vigor and Christopher Donnelly; and to my colleagues in the Department of War Studies and International Affairs.

The manuscript was typed intelligently and with great efficiency by Margaret Boyle, whose husband James played no small part in deciphering my handwriting. The Academy Librarian, Allan Shepperd, his successor John Hunt and their staff, have been especially helpful and tolerant in following up my many requests. The International Institute for Strategic Studies in London have allowed me to use their authoritative 'Military Balance' and their librarian Mrs Meryl Eady has been most helpful in my research. I am grateful to the editor of 'Janes Fighting Ships' for allowing me to quote the particulars which they publish on individual Soviet ships. The Royal Navy Public Relations Office have provided a wealth of photographic evidence from which we have chosen the jacket to the book; the endpaper map, depicting the Soviet naval bases, was drawn by Patrick Leeson.

Christopher Sinclair-Stevenson and John Henderson read the manuscript and have provided constructive criticism and advice in the production of the final text. Michael Wright, the Deputy Librarian at RMA Sandhurst, produced the index. Finally, a special thank you to my wife Pamela whose patience and fortitude sustained me throughout the research and writing of this book.

Sandhurst 1976   C.E.M.

. . . The flag of the Soviet Union flies over the oceans of the world. Sooner or later the United States will have to understand that it no longer has mastery of the seas . . .

SERGEI G. GORSHKOV
Admiral of the Fleet to
the Soviet Union
1974

Contents

Introduction

Alfred Thayer Mahan, the American strategist and military philosopher whose writing has had a profound influence on naval affairs since the latter part of the nineteenth century, believed seapower to be crucial to a nation's wealth and prestige. Since the Second World War, Britain's status as a great naval power has declined. Russia, meanwhile, has built up a naval capability of awe-inspiring dimensions.

It was the Soviet involvement in Angola in November 1975 which marked the real emergence of Russia as a world power, influential well beyond her own military bounds. She will no doubt take further opportunities, where they arise, to demonstrate her influence through her ever-increasing seapower.

Since the days of Peter the Great the Russians have proved themselves to be good shipbuilders, and their latest warships have earned the praise of Western experts; *Kiev*, for example, which combines beauty with menace, makes the *Ark Royal* seem positively matronly. Remembering that there could perhaps in time be six warships of this class, each complemented by cruiser and destroyer escorts and supported by a growing afloat support, it is not difficult to imagine such a force posing a real threat in a confrontation with the Free World.

Soviet seapower is not, of course, confined to the sea's surface; beneath it lurk the latest Soviet missile-armed nuclear-powered submarines. Ever-increasing numbers of the modern *Delta* and *Yankee* class vessels are deployed in support of the Soviet nuclear threat as a counter to the *Polaris* and *Poseidon* submarines of the Western navies. The Soviet submarine inventory also includes the excellent *Charlie* class hunter-killer with its sophisticated anti-ship missile system. The submarine forces of the confrontation powers are always deployed on a war footing in their operational cruises, and, whether strategic missile or hunter-killer, shadow their opponents in a game of life and death. Closer inshore, spy trawlers probe and monitor our vulnerable coastline, a constant reminder of increasing Soviet inquisitiveness. Finally, the Hammer and Sickle can be seen flying from the sterns of freighters in all the ports of the world, as the Soviet mercantile marine, free from the constraints of the profit motive, competes for the carriage of goods in what many experts see as an incipient form of economic warfare.

Outlined thus, Soviet naval power assumes frightening dimensions. A more realistic approach, however, must also take account of the limitations under which the Soviet Navy has to operate. Firstly, because of the sheer size of the country, the Russians have had to build four quite separate navies, based in Northern Waters, the Baltic, the Black Sea and the Pacific. Not only are these fleet bases separated by thousands of miles, but they contain subsidiary bases which are all, with one exception, dominated by unfriendly states in their exits and entrances.

Soviet warships carry a mix of weapons, and, since many of their operations are likely to occur beyond the cover of their own air force, they are prepared for a quick response to any threat. Obviously, confrontation with a Western fleet in the waters of the Atlantic, Mediterranean or Pacific, will automatically place the Russian navy at a serious disadvantage.

Although the *Kiev* is a ship of fine and revolutionary design, her capacity as an aircraft carrier is distinctly limited in comparison with American super carriers such as *Nimitz* or *Enterprise*. I contend that American naval strength is superior both in quality and quantity to that of the Soviet Union.

The United States is a maritime power with a long history of naval competence, and her principal allies share this distinction. Although it is true that the size and role of the Royal Navy have declined, its ships and the men who man them share a proud sense of tradition which is totally lacking in the Soviet fleet. Western techniques in anti-submarine warfare have established a lead over the Soviet Union which cannot be broken simply by the deployment of more ships. For all its recent advances, Soviet naval power has a chequered history, and even today remains the 'stepchild' of the more important and prestigious airforce and army.

So long as the West maintains its vigilance, the Soviet maritime threat can be kept in true and reasoned perspective. Mahan, however, believed it unlikely that a democracy could maintain a great naval power, since the population, by its very nature, is unwilling to pay the price of doing so. It is this feature of the naval balance which, in the long term, seems to me the most disturbing.

Part One

CHAPTER ONE

The Russian Maritime Heritage

Although the great inland waters and seas of Russia have always influenced its history, the development of a naval expertise and hence a maritime heritage dates from the reign of Peter the Great.[1] This haughty autocrat desired above all else to pursue the twin ambitions of centralising the government of Russia and expanding his domain into Central Europe and the Mediterranean. Amongst all the problems presented by such an ambitious policy, those concerned with the sea were invariably of primary importance. In his desire to take Russia into Europe he was confronted by the challenge of Sweden, an already well-established maritime power, which saw the Baltic as a Swedish Lake, while Russian expansion to the South-East could only be at the expense of Turkey.

It was the Swedish threat, in particular, which exposed the Russian need to develop a deep water navy for the first time. This, in turn, meant both sea-going ships and the sailors to man them, neither of which the Russians had. But one tradition which Russia did have, even in the seventeenth century was that of attracting foreigners who possessed the skills and knowledge of other civilizations. Peter the Great, who is often referred to as 'The Father of the Russian Navy" turned to those nations which possessed the seafaring tradition. At first this involved the Italian states whose sailors and shipwrights built and helped man a fleet of galleys. With this force the Russians captured Azov from the Turks in 1696,[2] the first naval victory in Russian history, and celebrated as such despite the fact that the Turks recaptured the port at a later date.[3]

To defeat the Turkish fleet with the traditional ship-of-war of the Mediterranean, the galley, was one thing, but against the Swedes

Peter also required the vessels of Western Europe, the ship-of-the-line. He travelled *incognito* to Holland and England as Peter Mihailoff, where he learnt the skills of the shipwright and recruited Englishmen to serve in his fleet. Thus Peter laid the foundations of another feature of the Russian maritime heritage, a naval link with England that was to last on and off to the October Revolution in 1917. By the turn of the century the naval base at Kronstadt had become operational and a school of mathematics and navigation had been established in Moscow; Peter the Great had thrown down the gauntlet to the Swedes and had staked his claims to the Baltic seas. A community of interests had been forged with the Danes, who had every reason to see the Swedes humbled, and between 1711–21 Peter waged a successful war in the Baltic.

When Peter the Great died in 1725 he left behind a Baltic Fleet which included fifty ships-of-the-line and more than 700 galleys. The Russian Maritime Regulations were administered through a Board of Admiralty and the hierarchy of the navy was clearly laid down by a table of ranks. But this new force was already displaying the impotency which was to become an inherent feature of Russian naval policy for many years to come. The Russian navy required the deep and personal commitments of the Tzars in order to maintain its efficiency for there was no mercantile marine which could complement the navy and provide it with sailors who had seagoing experience. Finally the navy placed too much reliance on mercenaries, especially as officers, which was to prove a fatal flaw in the Russian naval fabric.

The rather brittle and fragile nature of Peter's navy was clearly revealed in the years after his death. His successors showed little interest and the navy, eclipsed by the army, went into decline and disuse. The Turks recovered lost ground in the Black Sea and the Russian ships found that their quality allowed only for a limited role of coastal support to military operations. But this was also born out of necessity, and became a traditional element of Russian seapower.

One feature of the original navy which did remain a consistent theme of the eighteenth century was the use made of foreigners in Russian Naval service. Under the Empress Anna (1730–40) a Norwegian called Bredal commanded the naval effort against the Turks in the Mediterranean while another was a Dane, who had first taken service with Peter the Great and later became an explorer of renown. Vitus Jonassen Bering (1651–1741) was born in Jutland

and first recruited as a junior officer into the Russian Navy by the Norwegian-Russian Admiral Cruys. In 1724 he was sent by the Tzar to discover if Asia and America were connected by land. This first voyage convinced him that the two continents were not joined but his reports and findings were treated with scant regard by the government in Russia. Eventually, in 1783, the Empress Anna sponsored a second expedition which although strong enough on paper was inadequately supported. While Bering surveyed the hitherto unknown north coast his second-in-command explored the Kuril Islands and visited Japan. By 1741 Bering had charted the Aleutian Islands but with his crew suffering from the ravages of scurvy he was forced to land in the Gulf of Alaska. Worn out with the hardships of eight years of voyaging and wracked by scurvy he landed on Bering Island in November 1741 where he died of hunger, cold and disease. After his death the expedition simply disintegrated but the reports he wrote did find their way back to Russia and although in political terms never received the proper attention, at least were a major contribution to the geography of the northern region.

Under the Empress Catherine the Great,[4] the Russian Navy again resumed the full and personal attention of the sovereign. A new ship-building programme resulted in a tremendous expansion in the navy, and a mercantile marine was established but both of these developments once more revealed the Russian paucity in manpower and expertise. Foreigners again filled these depleted ranks with Catherine recruiting almost exclusively from the English and the Scots,[5] while Russian officers saw service in the Royal Navy. In 1769 a Russian fleet sailed from the Baltic under Count Orlov[6] to wage war on the Turkish squadrons in the Eastern Mediterranean and thereby draw the enemy away from the Black Sea. Although this was the first time that the Russians were to transfer seapower from one region to another, it was not the last, for it has become a major feature of Russian maritime strategy and reflects the often desperate predicament which the obstacle of geography presents to a country of this size.[7]

A combination and culmination of disasters forced Orlov to seek sanctuary in Plymouth. Scurvy, inexperienced sailors and leaking ships caused this inauspicious start to the expedition.[8] The ships were repaired, the sick landed and many English recruited to take their place. Rear-Admiral Sir John Elphinston, who had already distinguished himself in the Royal Navy, was given 'leave of absence' to command one of Orlov's squadrons. On the 5th July 1770 this cosmopolitan fleet fought a decisive, and indeed notorious, battle over the massed Turkish war galleys.[9] The Russian ships were out-numbered two to one, a feature in itself which is contrary to their tradition, but they annihilated the Turks in an engagement which many historians have claimed as one of the most complete victories in the annals of war at sea.[10]

Despite the magnitude of this victory, Catherine wisely refrained from maintaining a naval presence in the Eastern Mediterranean[11] for she shrewdly recognized that to have done so would have alarmed the British and French, who would both no doubt have bitterly resented such an intrusion into their own traditional areas.

With the Peace of Kuchuk Kainarji[12] Russian hegemony was assured for the time being and the navy once again entered a period of decline. But nevertheless it still attracted more than its fair share of colourful personalities, for that legend of American history John Paul Jones spent his last years of active life in Russian service.[13] After a spectacular career in the *Ranger*, raiding English shipping during the War of Independence, he had been sent as prize agent to Denmark; it was from there that, in 1778, he joined the Russian navy with the rank of Rear-Admiral. Although American historians would have it otherwise the Russians have always maintained that John Paul Jones made little contribution to their victories in the Black Sea. He returned to St. Petersburg in 1779 but only stayed there for a short while, since he became involved in scandal. He left the country in disgrace and returned to Paris where he died in 1782.

Renewed hostilities with Turkey in 1790 produced the first native-born Russian admiral of world stature. Feodr Feodorovich Ushakov achieved notable victories in the Mediterranean, one of which illustrated the same type of tactics that Nelson was later to use at the Nile; indeed, Soviet historians today have on a number of occasions referred to Admiral Ushakov as the 'Tutor of Nelson.'[14]

The Russian Navy in the period of the French Revolutionary and Napoleonic Wars was a rather hybrid affair for many of its officers were British and the only overseas bases it could use were British harbours. Russian units sailed from the Channel bases at Chatham and Portsmouth to take part in the blockade of the French coast,[15] while in the Mediterranean Admiral Ushakov captured the island of Corfu. The mentally unbalanced Tzar Paul I[16] provoked a quarrel with England when he accepted the title of the Grand

Master of the Knights of Malta.[17] The British resented this and the quarrel erupted into open violence when the island was captured in 1800 by the Royal Navy; Paul then seized British merchant shipping in Kronshtadt and conspired to deprive England of the invaluable Baltic timber trade. Nelson's victory at Copenhagen soon inspired a more cautious and pragmatic policy from the Tzar who returned the British merchantmen, paid compensation to their owners and renounced any claim to the titles of Malta.

Paul was assasinated in 1801 and replaced by his more amenable son Alexander[18] who, whilst not particularly interested in the Navy, sought to heal the breach caused by his father. Admiral Ushakov was now dead and his place was taken by Admiral Seniavin who had served his apprenticeship in the British Navy. Under his command Russian squadrons co-operated with Collingwood in the Mediterranean against their common foe, the Turks, and a number of Russian officers were with Nelson at the Battle of Trafalgar. Major reforms were introduced into the Russian naval organization by officers who had all been trained in the Royal Navy and in 1803 Captain Krusenten completed the first circumnavigation by a Russian. However, all this co-operation and mutual support between the two navies was fatally undermined by the Peace of Tilsit when Alexander was forced to accept French military hegemony and become allied to Napoleon. Admiral Seniavin and the Meditarranean squadrons, however, refused to fight their one-time allies, and instead sailed to Lisbon where the force was interned by the British.[19] Napoleon's invasion of Russia in 1812 restored the old relationship between the two navies and the Russians in particular, performed valuable service in co-operating with their armies and hounding the French lines of communication along the coastal reaches and inlets of the Southern Baltic shore.[20]. Russian ships once again appeared in the Mediterranean as part of the joint force while others operated in the North Sea with the Royal Navy. This happy state of affairs lasted until the peace of 1815.

The Eastern Mediterranean was the scene for one final major joint venture between the Royal Navies of Britain and Russia and once again the enemy was Turkey. The Battle of Navarino (1825)[21] was fought by naval contingents from Britain, Russia and France against a large but incredibly old-fashioned Turkish Fleet. This allied victory which resulted in the destruction of fifty Turkish ships assured the Greeks of independence when all else seemed lost, and at the same time led to the Sultan acknowledging Russian supremacy in the Black Sea. Russian historians would have us believe that the Russian squadron under Count Heyden not only bore the brunt of the fighting, while the British and French units held back, but by carrying the battle to the Turks ensured victory; such a hypothesis does not stand up to close examination.[22] Nevertheless the Russians have always been justly proud of this victory, for their squadron did fight with vigour and valour, and the squadron flagship *Azov* has been immortalised in the annals of their naval history. To this day there has always been a Russian warship called *Pamyat Azova* (*In memory of Azov*) and this ship always displays the badge of St. George, the Russian insignia for valour.

The Industrial Revolution and the age of steam heralded a period of comparative decline in the Russian navy which was destined to last more than a century. They were slow to adopt steam-powered ships,[23] this in itself reflecting the innate conservatism of Russian society, their lack of natural resources in coal and iron, and the paucity of labour and skilled craftsmen. In the Crimean War the Russian Navy was hopelessly out-matched both in the Black Sea and the Baltic so that the sailors were used on land as infantry while the warships were laid up in their home ports.[24] Only on rare occasions did the ships venture out and even then scuttled back behind the shelter of their garrison artillery at the first sign of the Royal Navy. In the final quarter of the century there was some revival of interest in the fleets, the Tzar Alexander II appointed his brother as Minister of Marine. This resulted in a prototype ironclad being imported from England and the eventual appearance of a small squadron of screw-driven warships in the Baltic, but the standard of maintenance was such that the ships had only an indifferent performance, while their design lagged far behind the more progressive navies.[25]

By the turn of the century the navy had begun to show some improvements under Tzar Alexander III and his son Nicholas II: the navy was encouraged to learn from others and new methods were copied from the naval powers, especially the Germans. However all this was dissipated in a ruinous war with Japan; the Russo-Japanese war is probably chiefly remembered for the almost total defeat of the Imperial Navy at the Battle of Tsushima.

Tzar Nicholas introduced an acquisitive foreign policy in the Far East which meant that the Pacific Fleet should operate out of the secure base of a warm water port. Such a policy was bound to result in a collision with the rapidly emerging naval power of Japan. The Russians found their base in Port Arthur which the Japanese had been forced to return to China in 1895; the Chinese with a little pressure allowed the Russians to garrison this base under the cynical guise of protecting them from the further ravages of Japan. For the first time in their history the Russians possessed two viable bases for their Pacific Fleet, in Vladivostock and Port Arthur, and this represented a direct challenge to Japanese ambitions for the naval hegemony of the North Pacific.

The Japanese war aim was clear and explicit. They needed to bottle up the Russian squadrons in their respective bases and then destroy each in turn with an overwhelming show of force. To this end the Japanese prepared secretly for war and then, in a style reminscent of a later occasion, struck swiftly and without warning early in 1904.[26] Japanese mine-laying proved almost immediately successful for when the Russians sailed out from Port Arthur in April to meet the Japanese challenge their flagship the *Petropavlousk* was enticed onto a minefield and sank, taking almost the full complement and their Admiral, Makharoff to the bottom.[27] By August of that year the Russian naval presence was practically destroyed. While the Imperial Japanese Army laid seige to Port Arthur from the landward side, their naval squadron defeated the Russian fleet twenty miles out,[28] the few vessels that survived struggled back into the harbour. In the meanwhile the squadron at Vladivostock was defeated by the Japanese fleet under Admiral Kamimura as it tried to reach Port Arthur.[29] In five short months the Japanese had thus secured control over the Northern Pacific and had completely destroyed the Russian squadrons as a viable naval force. It is ironic that the architect of this brilliant episode in Japanese history, Admiral Togo, was an officer who had studied the art of naval warfare in England and whose major victory over the Russians, which was still to come, was to earn him the immortal title of the 'Nelson of the East'.

Tzar Nicholas II prided himself on being a European and thus this defeat of his navy by an oriental power represented a double humiliation as well as thwarting his ambitions in the Pacific. He therefore decided to restore the balance and regain his tarnished reputation by transferring his only remaining fleet from the Baltic to the Northern Pacific, and so began what must be regarded as one of the most bizarre episodes in naval history. Nicholas appointed Admiral Rozhestvenski to command this expedition, at fifty-six a relatively young officer who owed his rapid promotion to his dashing exploits as a torpedo boat commander when fighting against the Turks. The spearhead of the Baltic fleet was built around four new battleships, which were not really operational, manned by novice crews. The rest of the fighting ships (together with the fleet support and colliers) were vessels that already belonged to a bygone age, old ships armed with obsolescent guns and poor crews.

Rozhestvenski intended to work up his fleet during the voyage to the Pacific, but even as he sailed from the Baltic[30] alarmist (and totally unfounded) reports warned him that Japanese torpedo boats, which had been shipped to England, were already lying in wait in the North Sea. This jittery Russian fleet fired on a Swedish merchant ship and the occasional German fishing vessel in the Baltic; it was hardly surprising therefore, that when it came upon British trawlers operating in the fishing grounds off the Dogger Bank, in the dead of night, that 'all hell should break loose'.[31] At point-blank range, as mass hysteria gripped the Russian ships, broadsides poured into the trawlers, although British loss of life would have been much greater if the Russian gunnery had been even half-way efficient. Nevertheless by the time the Russians had realised their mistake the damage had been done; although only one trawler actually sank, a number of lives were lost and the resultant indignation and sense of outrage in England pushed the two countries to the brink of war. Royal Naval units shadowed the Russian fleet through the English channel and out into the open seas as far as Tangier, with their main armament trained on this hapless Russian Force. At the Mediterranean the Russian fleet divided, the older units proceeded to the Indian Ocean via the Suez Canal while Rozhestvenski took his main squadron the additional 10,000 miles around the Cape of Good Hope. In the New Year of 1905 the units rendezvoused at Madagascar where the fleet waited for two months for the reinforcements of the Black Sea fleet and for colliers and auxiliaries to replenish the much depleted bunkers.[32] This period of enforced delay and inactivity in an unhealthy and disease-ridden anchorage played havoc with Russian morale and efficiency.

It was while they were off Madagascar that news was received of the Fall of Port Arthur.[33] Rozhestvenski dared not turn back and so the nearest haven was Vladivostock, a voyage in itself of many thousands of miles through waters unknown to the navigators, and between them and safety was the Japanese fleet under Togo. In March new units joined up with the fleet at Madagascar, including the battleship *Nikokai I* and the force set out across the Indian Ocean. In early April the Royal Navy shadowed the Russian fleet as it passed within sight of Singapore[34] on the way to Kamranh Bay in Cochin China where Rozhestvenski intended to make his final landfall and complete his preparations before undertaking the last leg of this remarkable voyage to Vladivostock. At Kamranh Bay a reinforcement reached the Russian Admiral in the form of a second squadron of new fast battleships from the Baltic fleet, which had not even been completed when the original force first sailed.[35] On the 14th May 1905 this enormous armada set sail for its rendezvous with destiny and the waiting Japanese. The Russians had already completed an incredible voyage, but the ships were now badly in need of a major refit, the crews were stale and tired and the strain of command was already beginning to exert a fatal influence over Admiral Rozhestvenski. The Japanese, on the other hand, had been able to follow the Russian movement from the telegraph of the press agencies, while the precise details were passed on by the friendly British. The Japanese ships had been refitted and replenished, their crews were well trained, rested and, above all, under the inspired leadership of their dynamic commander.

Rozhestvenski's force made sedate passage northwards passing through the Bashi Channel between the Philippines and Formosa, his more modern and faster warships fatally inhibited by the pace of the older and slower brethren. Although lacking any precise information of the Japanese deployment, location or strength, Rozhestvenski was sanguine enough to appreciate that he must now fight his way through to Vladivostock. Accordingly he detached his auxiliaries from the main force at Shanghai where they were to await events. From Shanghai northwards there were a number of routes the Russians could take to reach Vladivostock, but Admiral Togo was convinced that the Russians must come through the Tsushima passage, for it represented the most direct course, and he deployed his force accordingly. Rozhestvenski was indeed heading for the passage and was timing his run to clear this stretch of water in daylight for he knew that he could not trust the competence of his ships' navigators to make the passage at night.

On the 27th May 1905[36] thirty-seven Russian warships steamed through the Tsushima passage at their best speed of eleven knots;

the battle force was deployed in two parallel lines, cruisers scouted ahead while the few essential auxiliaries brought up the rear escorted by the older vessels. The Japanese received word of the Russian movements from their scouting cruisers and Togo deployed his force from its anchorage at Masampo Bay in Korea in good time to contest the Russian passage. The Japanese were, on paper, heavily out-numbered but had the advantage of superior fire-power and speed; this allowed Togo to complete the classic manoeuvre of naval warfare by crossing the 'T' with his battleships while his armoured cruisers harried the Russian flanks.

Battle opened at a range of 9,500 yards in the early afternoon and the Japanese broadsides wrought havoc on the Russian battle-ships in the van of the line who could offer only poor response with their forward firing guns. Most of the many excellent accounts of this engagement are all based on the report of a British naval officer who with the sang-froid typical of his breed, observed events from a deck chair on the Japanese flagship's quarterdeck! By the late afternoon the Japanese victory was assured. The Russian battleships were either sunk or disabled, their squadron commanders had lost all control, and indeed the wounded Admiral Rozhestvenski was captured as he tried to run for Vladivostock in a fast destroyer after his own flagship had been sunk.[37] As night fell those Russian vessels that had somehow survived the holocaust of fire were harried and pursued by the lighter units of the Japanese navy while the disabled battleships were finished off by Togo's cruisers. Only one small cruiser, the *Almaz*, reached Vladivostock with two attendant destroyers while three other cruisers sought sanctuary in Manila.[38]

The maritime powers hastened to digest the lessons of Tsushima and almost all learned the wrong ones.[39] For Russia, humiliation and defeat was even further endorsed as the Japanese revived the old custom of incorporating the spoils into their own fleet. Eastern power had displayed its ability to master Western technology, but few nations seemed to take cognizance of that fact.

Notes

1. Peter I, the Great (1672–1725).
2. The Russian flotillas were under the Command of Lefort, a Swiss Admiral.
3. *Azov* was recaptured in 1711 by the Turks and the Russian Black Sea Fleet was destroyed.

4. Empress Catherine, the Great, (1729–96).

5. Fred T. Jane claims in *The Imperial Russian Navy* (W. Thacker & Co., 1904) that almost half the active list were British. The officers were serving Royal Navy officers on secondment to the Russian Navy.

6. Orlov, a court favourite, travelled overland, joining the Fleet at Leghorn; until his arrival the first squadron and overall command was under Admiral Spiridov.

7. This Baltic squadron was reinforced by two frigates that sailed from the White Sea Fleet at Archangel.

8. Over 300 Russians died on the way to England and 600 were landed in British ports as too sick to be of any further service. For more detailed information see David Woodward, *The Russian at Sea* (William Kimber & Co. Ltd.: London, 1965).

9. The Battle of Tchesma. The Russian force was nine ships-of-the-line, three frigates and a bomb vessel. The Turkish strength was some twenty ships, including ships-of-the-line and frigates.

10. The final part of the victory was achieved by sending fire ships, commanded by Commodore Greig RN, into the crowded Turkish moorings in Tchesma Harbour.

11. Even so, with the Turkish Mediterranean Fleet destroyed, the Russian squadrons went on to blockade the Dardanelles.

12. July 1774. A Treaty which gave the Russians the ports of Azov, Taganrog, Kertch and Kinbarn. In addition the Crimea was declared nominally independent, but the Russians were able to annexe it in 1783. The Russians lost little time in the construction of Sevastopol as their main naval base in the Black Sea.

13. His elevation to flag-rank was loudly criticised by his colleagues, and one-time enemies, British naval officers on secondment.

14. A battle which began off Temdra and ended off Hadjibey—near to the mouth of the Danube—and in which Ushakov used a squadron of three frigates as a detached force; the Russians also claim that Nelson's stratagem of dividing the British Fleet into two divisions at Trafalgar was a copy of this device. Nelson and Ushakov served together in the Mediterranean; the Russian was treated with that special contempt that Nelson reserved for foreigners!

15. Including participation in the combined operations of the Duke of York's campaign along the Dutch Coast and garrison duty in the Channel Islands.

16. One of the aspects of Paul's madness was a mania for uniforms. He designed uniforms (all of which bore a strange resemblance to Prussian styles of half a century before) for all his forces and palace officials. Among the most bizarre was a new naval uniform which was to remain unchanged for the next century and was green in colour.

17. Partly caused by his fetish for uniforms.

18. Alexander I (1777–1825).

19. Though it was a different tale in the Baltic where Britain combined with the Swedes against Russia. A number of naval actions were fought, mostly small scale or single ships.

20. Once again British officers were seconded to the Russian Navy. Captain T. B. Martin RN had adventures similar to those which befell C. S. Forester's hero, Hornblower, in *The Commodore*.

21. The Battle of Navarino was the last battle fought between sailing ships-of-the-line. The Russian contingent was commanded by a German emigré, Admiral Heyden, and consisted of 4 ships-of-the-line and 4 frigates. The Supreme Allied Commander was Admiral Sir Edward Codrington RN who flew his flag on the 84-gun *Asia*. He had 2 other British ships-of-the-line, 2 frigates and 2 sloops. The French squadron was 3 ships-of-the-line and 2 frigates. Thus the total allied strength was 19 warships with 1,190 guns against a Turkish line of battle force of 20 ships (1,150 guns).

22. The Russian squadron was the last of the combined fleet to join battle and engaged the weakest part of the Turkish line. Though at one stage five Turkish warships concentrated upon the Russian flagship Azov and it did have the highest casualties among the allies: ninety-one killed and wounded.

23. Although the first Russian steam warship *Skoryi* was laid down in 1817.

24. The Russian squadron in Sevastopol was scuttled. The Anglo-French sent a squadron to attack the Russian Pacific base at Petro Pavlovsk (Vladivostock did not exist, and its territory was not part of Russia) but it proved to be pretty disastrous. China ceded Amur Province to Russia in 1859.

25. However, in 1863 two Russian squadrons sailed the Atlantic from their Baltic Base. One squadron visited New York and the other San Francisco.

26. The Russian First Pacific Squadron was on a war-footing and at anchor in the roadstead to Port Arthur when on the night of 8th February, Japanese destroyers delivered a devastating torpedo attack; two out of seven battleships, together with a light cruiser, were damaged. The Japanese had broken off diplomatic relations but had not made a formal declaration of war at the time of this attack.

27. The flagship sank in under two minutes, seven officers and seventy-three men were saved out of her complement of 715. The battleship *Pobieda* followed its leader onto the minefield and pandemonium broke out in the fleet with ships firing at one another. After order was restored it withdrew rather ignominiously into harbour.

28. The Battle of Shantung or the Battle of the Yellow Sea, 10th August 1905.

29. Kamimura in command of the Japanese Armoured Cruisers sank one Russian cruiser and badly damaged two others in this engagement in the Korean Straits, just north of Tsushima, on 14th August 1905. After this defeat the Vladivostock squadron ceased to exist.

30. The squadron sailed from Libau on 15th October 1905.

31. The night of 21/22nd October. The Russians did agree to pay compensation for this incident.

32. It could take anything up to twenty-four hours of non-stop labour to coal a battleship; in the Tropics this would mean working in temperatures of 115 degrees.

33. The island of Madagascar, French-owned, where the Russians in contravention of international law received full hospitality from the local authorities. The Russians remained off Madagascar for three months; their anchorage was at Sainte Marie in the north-west. The Fleet sailed on 16 March on the 4,700 mile voyage to the French colonies in Indo-China. The Fleet coaled at sea, an almost unique operation in those days.

34. April 8th.

35. By all accounts Rozhestvenski had done his best to avoid this reinforcing squadron, realising that its ancient cruisers would reduce the effectiveness of his fighting force.

36. The anniversary of the Coronation of the Tzar and Tzarina.

37. The flagship *Suvarov* fought to the very end, with only one twelve-pounder gun in action, all the remaining sixty-four guns were knocked out.

38. This included the *Aurora*, a cruiser which figured prominently in the opening stages of the October Revolution. Rozhestvenski, his deputy Nebogatov and his staff were tried by Court Martial on their release from a Japanese Prison Camp. The Admiral was acquitted, though he attempted to assume the blame, but his staff received heavy prison sentences. The Admiral died in 1909.

39. Included in any list of wrong lessons learned would be the use of high explosive rather than armour-piercing shells (the British were to pay heavily for this at Jutland) and the inclusion of armoured cruisers in the battle line.

CHAPTER TWO

The Red Navy

The Imperial Navy never really recovered from the calamities of the war with Japan. Tzar Nicholas did order a new programme of reconstruction but the outbreak of the Great War saw the navy still in the process of recovery. In 1912 a new fleet was beginning to emerge in the Baltic, where British and French engineers were building marine propulsion plants while the Germans helped with blue prints and specifications for a range of warships from dreadnoughts to destroyers.[1] The Revolution in 1905 had also left its mark on the fleet, particularly in the Baltic, and although episodes such as the 'Battleship Potemkin' have been popularised, what was more important was the spread of revolutionary ideals through the fleet. Many of the petty officers and senior ratings were recruited into the Party at this time which gave them a position of advantage from which to spread the word as well as undermining the relationship between these men, the backbone of any fleet, and the regular officer corps.

For most of the Great War there was little large-scale naval activity in the Baltic, and nothing which approached a major fleet engagement. The Germans for their part concentrated the bulk of their front-line strength and main battle fleet against the British fleet in the North Sea and had little to spare in terms of capital units for any Baltic scenario.[2] The Russian navy, as we have seen, was still working up to a new peak of operational efficiency and so had to content itself with protecting the maritime approaches to the capital at St. Petersburg and defending the Gulf of Finland.

Thus in terms of capital ships and fleet engagements the Baltic presented a picture of stability through powerlessness throughout the long years of the First World War.[3] The pattern of naval activity was dictated by the smaller units, destroyers and gunboats, which carried out infrequent raids against their opponent's bases or on the army's line of communication. When it strayed near the coast and within gun range, coastal convoys also came in for the occasional sortie if the target was tempting enough. Both sides expended a lot of effort and showed considerable ingenuity in minelaying; the mine caused more casualties, both in ships and men, than any other in this theatre of operations.[4]

In contrast the Russian fleet operations in the Black Sea[5] present an entirely different picture. The defeat by the Japanese had only influenced this fleet indirectly, thus the morale and professional efficiency of the ships and the crews was of a very high order when hostilities began with Turkey. The shipyards had produced a number of new dreadnoughts, modern cruisers and fast destroyers which were more than a match for the obsolescent vessels of their traditional Turkish adversary. The arrival of the German battle-cruiser *Goeben* with her attendant cruiser the *Breslau*, in Turkish waters after they had successfully eluded British pursuit did restore some of the balance, but in no way intimidated the Russian sailors. Russian warships put to sea on numerous occasions throughout the war and their battleships proved more than a match for the German and Turkish forces. The arrival of large German U-boats in the theatre did take some of the dash out of the Russians and install some prudence, but nevertheless in the period right up to the Peace in April 1918 the Russian Navy performed sterling work in the Black Sea.

The enforced inactivity of the battleships and cruisers in the Baltic ports helped foster a feeling of resentment and frustration amongst the bored crews. By 1916, except for minelaying operations, the only real naval activity was submarine warfare, this because of the example set by a small force of British submarines which was sent into the Baltic to instill the art into their Russian allies. Submarine warfare was in an embryonic form until the arrival of the British but the Russians learned fast and the joint force soon scored a number of notable successes which included sinking the German battle-cruiser *Moltke*. But this was not enough to offset the process of decay in the rest of the fleet, for the petty officers had done their work well and by 1917 the Baltic Fleet was more than ready to fulfil its allotted role in the Revolution.[6] The cruiser *Aurora* played its now famous part in the October events by firing on the Winter

Palace in Petrograd[7] and thus signalling the start of the Revolution. Throughout the fleet the petty officers and senior ratings quickly usurped the positions and commands of the Tzarist officers and then led the sailors ashore to become the 'shock-troops' of Revolution.

Lenin disbanded the Tzarist fleet and on the 12th February 1918 created the 'Socialist Worker Peasant Fleet', but this emotive and even grandiose label did not in itself remove the abuses and maladies which had been rampant in the fleet for so long. Throughout the subsequent period of Civil War the sailors from Kronshtadt were in the forefront of the Bolshevik struggles against the forces of reaction and counter-revolution, but nothing was done to restore the efficiency or quality of the fleet; instead, the sense of grievance grew. As the Civil War drew to a close the sailors, who now felt that they occupied a special place in the Revolution, demanded reform and reconstruction of the Baltic Fleet, but their cries fell on deaf ears and so by a strange, ironic quirk of fate became in turn the focus of revolt.

On 1st March 1921 the new Soviet Republic was severely shaken by the outbreak of the Kronshtadt naval uprising. At first the mutineers proved to be highly successful; they secured the naval base and easily repulsed the assaults of loyal government troops as they stormed the defences from across the frozen wastes of the Gulf of Finland. Eventually strategem and guile saw the defences breached and the Red Guard took Kronshtadt after two days of bitter street fighting. On the heels of the advancing government troops came the Cheka, the dreaded secret police, and those sailors of the original 6,000 who survived were summarily executed by firing squads.

The Soviet Navy took many years to recover from the Kronshtadt Naval Mutiny, and one cannot escape the conclusion that the paucity of funds devoted by the Kremlin to the naval vote reflected, for a number of years, not just a lack of confidence in their sea-power, but also a desire to punish those who would seek to dispute the dictates of Central Government.[8] The navy was purged of many of its long service ratings and their places filled by members of the Komsomol, the 'volunteer' Communist Youth League. Precise figures are difficult to find but it would seem that some twenty per cent of the sailors were removed immediately and that by 1928 some seventy per cent of the Baltic Fleet were Komsomol members. The officer corps was, however, still largely Tzarist in origin for like the Red Army, it seemed that the Central Government appreciated the need to have experienced professional serving officers; revolutionary zeal was not yet seen as a substitute for technical competence. But life for these one-time servants of the Tzar could not have been easy, for they were under constant surveillance by the Cheka, frequently called before Tribunals where their loyalty was scrutinised and gradually replaced as new officers of the Revolution completed their training and became available for service.

The legacies of the Tzarist past were not just confined to the officer corps in the Red Navy; the ships were the same[9] for there was no new shipbuilding programme, and the teachings of the past survived into the Revolutionary period. There was, at first, no attempt to implement a radical new naval doctrine and strategy in the light of Marxist concepts, and so the old skills and principles continued to be taught at the two naval academies, the Voroshilov Naval War College and the Frunze Naval Academy in Leningrad. Those professors who had survived the traumas of the Revolution taught a slightly modified version of Mahan's theories on the 'Command of Sea' to a new generation of Soviet naval officers and cadets. This old school of thought or strategy still saw the need to exercise control or command of the maritime approaches to Russia. The composition of naval forces deemed necessary to execute this task was likewise seen in a classical sense of a balanced force of battleships, cruisers and destroyers. 'Revolutionary' weapon systems based on the aircraft and the submarine were largely ignored by the Soviet professors who proposed instead a naval construction programme that in terms of cost alone, and ignoring the relevance of expertise, was totally beyond the resources of the new state.[10] In practice the fleet in the Baltic was so weak that the most it could have done in the event of war would have been to adopt a strategy of passive defence, using nearly immobile ships as floating batteries and the few coastal fortifications which had survived the ravages of revolution and the subsequent period of neglect. In this sense the Soviet Navy more precisely conformed to Mahan's theories on the 'Fortress Fleet'.

If the Red Navy saw any foe who was at all likely to challenge them in the early Twenties it was the Royal Navy, with memories still fresh of the British intervention on the side of the White Russians during the Civil War. Accordingly some coastal forts in the Baltic region were rearmed with batteries which could outgun the main armament of the opposing battle fleet; Kronstadt naval base was repaired after the ravages of the March coup, some new batteries were mounted and a minefield laid in the Gulf of Finland. The only naval vessels which were operational in the Baltic were one dreadnought which could have been utilized as a floating battery, a modest posse of eight destroyers, a couple of submarines and a few light craft.

In the Black Sea the situation was even more precarious. Practically all the heavy units, the dreadnoughts and cruisers, which had performed so well in the Great War had sided with the White Russian forces in the Civil War. These ships followed their leader, General Pyotr Mikolayevich, into exile and internment just prior to the final victory of the Communist forces, when they sailed to the Tunisian Port of Bizerte and sought sanctuary from the French.[11] This meant that the Soviet naval defence of the vital regions of the Black Sea was centred once more on minefields with a few submarines and gunboats to provide a more active force. There were also some light naval forces deployed in the Caspian Sea to counter the British presence in Persia while elsewhere, in the Pacific and Northern Waters, no serious attempt was made to reconstitute a naval presence until the early Thirties.

Gradually the Tzarist officers tried to move away from the tenets of the 'fortress fleet' and in accordance with the teaching of the 'old school' of strategists adopted an offensive—or more precisely an 'active defence'–concept in which the light surface units practised operations away from their bases towards the mouth of the Gulf of Finland.[12] Despite the financial stringencies of a nearly bankrupt government, which was still obsessed by the Kronshtadt mutiny, two old battleships reappeared in 1927 and exercised in the Baltic Sea as the embryo of a new battle line. Although this represents a major achievement on their part it does mark the end of the Tzarist influence on the Soviet Navy. More and more younger officers were now graduating from the Naval Academies and their rapid promotion to positions of command and influence swamped the views of the traditionalists. These officers, imbued with revolutionary zeal, distrusted the traditional naval doctrines based on experiences learned directly from war at sea and lessons assimilated from those of other navies. Instead they sought, as the 'Young School' of strategy, to propagate a new doctrine of naval warfare which reflected the environment of their own formative years and training. This new doctrine was derived from a mixture of Marxist-Leninist teachings on dialectic materialism and the principles of partisan warfare. For the 'Young School' the instrument of partisan warfare and revolutionary war at sea was to be the submarine which they believed had now replaced the battleship as the main strike force of the fleet. They saw the pitched battles of Tsushima and Jutland as things of the past, and instead saw the submarine, used in large numbers and ably supported by fast surface craft and naval aircraft, as the true components of the modern twentieth-century navy. Their arguments had the force of revolutionary zeal which carried influence and favour in the corridors of the Kremlin, but their real attraction was the fact that such a fleet would be cheap to build and maintain. The 'Old School' of strategists, some of whom still taught in the Naval Academies, were purged for their heresy and many paid the ultimate price for the 'obduracy of their reactionary thoughts'.

The Soviet Second Five Year Plan, which began on the 1st January 1933,[13] earmarked a substantial proportion of the naval vote for submarine construction with the result that by 1937 the Soviet Navy boasted the largest force of submarines in the world. Stalin, however, who had finally secured total control through the bloody and ruthless purges of the officer corps in the army and navy, was never completely committed to the 'Young School' and hedged his bet by ordering the construction of heavy cruisers and the refitting of three of the Tzarist dreadnoughts during the latter stages of the Five Year Plan. Indeed the doubts which he felt about the ability of a navy biased so heavily in favour of submarines were borne out by the events of the Spanish Civil War in 1937. Russian attempts to sponsor the cause of the Republicans in Spain, particularly when the Germans and Italians espoused the Nationalists under Franco, revealed the pressing need to deploy a balanced surface fleet to counter the other side. The submarine proved to be of little value as either a purveyor of presence or an instrument of blockade off the coast of Spain, while the surface units which were available could not counter the naval presence of the German and Italian navies.

Stalin seemed to have been determined to provide the Soviet Union with a navy which would restore her to a position of primacy among the maritime powers of the world. To this end the Third Five Year Programme envisaged the construction of a powerful and balanced surface fleet;[14] one which would command respect from others and serve as a real extension of Soviet diplomacy. Russian shipyards began immediately in 1938 to construct the cruisers and destroyers ordered by the government, but capital ships presented a major problem. There were no Russian slipways capable of constructing battleships over 30,000 tons, the steel works had no experience in producing high grade armoured plate, and the service industries when confronted with the need to provide fire control systems, communications networks, and modern gunnery, found the level of technology beyond their experience.

The Russian Government turned to the United States for help and advice in the construction of those capital ships which were beyond their own capabilities. There is no precise information available on what the Russians were really after but it does seem that they were looking for technical advice on the construction of three new battleships to be built in Russia when the slipways were ready, and for another, a 'super battleship' to be constructed in the United States. Negotiations dragged on for more than two years without much real progress until the European crisis, which erupted in 1939, brought an abrupt end to Russian aspirations. The Carp Corporation, a shipbuilding consortium owned by a naturalised American called Henry Carp, whose sister was married to the Soviet Premier Molotov, was used by the Russians to lobby support in the Government. In principle Molotov was in favour of such a venture on the grounds that any American refusal would simply drive the Russians further into the German Camp. The real problem was caused by the doubts expressed by Henry Carp as to whether, even with American assistance, the Russians had the necessary knowledge and expertise to construct their own battleships. The question of the battleship to be constructed in the United States presented a different problem, of a political nature, for Stalin ordered a battleship which exceeded the treaty limits as laid down in the Washington Naval Agreements.

It would also seem that an aircraft carrier was included on Stalin's 'shopping list' in America. In this case the negotiations did not progress very far since Stalin wanted information and blue prints of the latest type of American carriers that were still at the time under construction. In 1939 a Soviet naval delegation was sent to the United States to try to resolve the impasse but it was all to no avail and the Russians looked to their own means to provide the new capital ships. It is reasonably certain that two battleship keels were laid down in Leningrad in early 1940 and a third in Nikolayevsk. Nothing more was heard of the aircraft carrier project and Western historians have since been highly critical of

Stalin's failure to ensure the construction of a balanced surface force. That Stalin intended Russia to have a navy of world stature is beyond doubt and in this sense the outbreak of the Second World War in simple terms imposed an interlude on this ambitious programme. Nevertheless the Soviet Naval programme as it stood on the eve of war reflected naval trends world-wide; the Washington Naval Limits had expired in 1936 and all the leading navies were deeply involved in constructing new and even bigger warships. Stalin realised by the events in Spain, as much as anywhere else, that in order for diplomacy to succeed Russia must have a navy that will at least rank with those of the major maritime powers. As early as 1932 and 1935 respectively the Russians had reconstituted their naval squadrons in the Artic and the Pacific and this also placed a new imperative on the need to deploy ocean-going ships. With four fleet areas to sustain there was a need to reinforce one or other as the occasion arose, and this required that Soviet vessels should move out of the claustrophobic confines of the Black and Baltic Seas onto the oceans of the world. Long and difficult voyages of this nature could only be undertaken by a deep sea navy.

The failure of the Russians to appreciate the need for aircraft carriers before the Second World War has been over-criticised in the West. In this particular period only the Japanese Navy had produced carriers in the correct proportion to their surface forces whilst the Americans and the British were trying desperately to compensate for the years of neglect with a series of emergency programmes. The German and Italian navies saw their surface units operating within range of land-based air support or in the narrower confines of the Mediterranean so that neither really took seriously the need for carriers. The British proved that carrier operations in the confined waters of the Mediterranean can on occasions be successful but also very expensive; the Malta convoys were given carrier support but that failed to counter the overwhelming effect of land-based aircraft. It is this writer's contention that even if Russia had an aircraft carrier in either the Black Sea or the Baltic during the Second World War it would have proved in all probability quite ineffective against the crushing air superiority which the Luftwaffe secured in the early months of the war in Eastern Europe.

'Operation Barbarossa' and the invasion of Russia in June 1941 brought to an abrupt end the Soviet naval construction programme;

very few of the new ships ordered under the Five Year Plan were completed, let alone operational. The purges of the officer corps in the mid-thirties and the confusion over strategies and schools of thought found the navy without experienced and competent commanders and lacking in direction and purpose.[15] The rapid pace of the Panzer thrust across the Northern reaches of the old Baltic States deprived the Soviet Navy of bases from which to operate and airfields from which they could obtain air support. By the autumn of 1941 the bulk of the Soviet Baltic Fleet was bottled up in its naval bases at Kronshtadt and the Neva River. Those larger units which survived the pounding from the Luftwaffe were rapidly converted into floating batteries and their surplus crews drafted into the Red Army in the desperate defence of Leningrad. For a while the submarines braved the German minefields and attempted to carry the war to the enemy; they fought with bravery but little skill. After some initial successes against coastal shipping, the Germans deployed fast destroyers equipped with sophisticated anti-submarine warfare techniques which proved more than a match for the Russian commanders in the narrow shoal waters of the Baltic.

In the more Northern waters the outbreak of war found a significant force of Russian warships deployed in Murmansk and the Kola Inlet,[16] and it was these units together with a small submarine force which were supposed to co-operate with the Britis hand American navies. All Western naval histories of the Second World War criticise and condemn the Russian naval effort in this theatre of operations. It was only on rare occasions that the Soviet ships made sorties from the security of their bases to help augment the critically over-stretched escorts of the Artic convoys. The Russian ships were obviously acting under the orders of their High Command not to risk damage from enemy attack or to fraternise with the Western navies; very few facilities were provided in the Russian bases for their allies, and the Soviet force engendered a spirit of suspicion and frustration, which angered and embittered their comrades-in-arms in this particularly vicious theatre of operations.

On the Southern Front the Soviet Navy appeared to be particularly strong,[17] especially as the Germans and their Balkan allies could muster only naval forces of an indifferent quality.[18] However, this arena illustrated once again the folly of operating naval units at sea without an adequate air umbrella; the Luftwaffe with their mastery of the skies wrought havoc among those Russian ships that dared to put to sea. The advancing Wehrmacht captured the Russian naval bases in the Crimea[19] and by the end of 1942 the surviving ships could only operate out of the cramped harbours of Batum, Poti and Sukhumi in the Southern Caucasus.

It took a long time for the Russian Navy to move over to the offensive and the Germans were in full retreat before the naval units in both the Baltic and Black Seas attempted any harassment of their lines of communication. The Luftwaffe had been driven from the skies, and the Soviet airforce completely dominated the battle fronts and yet the Russian navy showed a marked reluctance to become involved. On a number of occasions, in both theatres of operation, the Germans evacuated large numbers of troops by sea using hastily improvised shipping and without escort. The Red Navy confined its activities to the occasional amphibious raid and night attack, and for the most part it fulfilled the traditional function of protecting the maritime flanks of the land armies.

In the Far East the Soviet Pacific Fleet comprised two of the new heavy cruisers, some twenty destroyers and escort vessels and a large force of more than sixty submarines. For the greater part of the war these ships were used to watch their traditional Japanese enemy. By the time the Russians declared war on Japan in August 1945 their opponent's navy had been effectively swept from the seas by the American Pacific Fleet. Consequently the Red Navy was used only to secure those territories which the Russians were to receive for the ten days of arduous warfare waged against Japan. Task forces consequently secured the surrender of Japanese troops on Southern Sakhalin and some of the Kuril Islands while other ships made landings on the shores of Northern Korea.

This account of the history and development of the Russian navy since the seventeenth century does show a country capable of producing good ships and good seamen, yet in the period of the Second World War the navy displayed neither skill nor success in its conduct of operations.[20] Even the post-war historians and propagandists have shown a marked reticence to promote the image of 'the fighting navy' in any way which was comparable to their portrayals of the Red Army and Air Force. Yet it does seem that the indifferent achievements of the Soviet Navy cannot solely be dismissed in terms of incompetence, poor command and lack of good seamanship, though these were undoubtedly contributing factors.

In the initial stages of the war the naval operations were no worse than the other services which in proportion suffered less loss of capital equipment and manpower. However, unlike the Army and the Air Force, there was no hinterland into which the navy could retreat and rebuild. The loss of its harbours and construction yards proved to be a crippling blow which could not be replaced without reconquest, although the British and Americans did make some gestures towards re-equipping the Russian navy. Army divisions and air squadrons could be trained in areas secure from enemy attack, while the navy had constantly to remain in the front line. By the time that the Germans were in full retreat pursued by fresh well-trained and well-equipped Soviet Tank divisions, the naval vessels were in need of repair and refit. Finally although many opportunities to seize the initiative were forfeited it should be remembered that the naval units came under the control of the 'Front Commanders', Army Generals deeply embroiled in the land battle and with neither the time nor inclination to appreciate the finer points of naval tactics and doctrine.

Thus Western comment on the Soviet Navy's role and performance during the Second World War is over-critical and fails to acknowledge the basic limitations under which the Russian sailors had to operate. Neither, of course, can one accept the Soviet version of events, especially those articles which have recently appeared in Western journals.

Notes

1. The battleship programme envisaged the type of warship that was not due to appear in most other navies for at least another twenty years, four 32,000 ton battleships which combined the armament of battleships with the speed of battlecruisers. In addition four new light cruisers (7,000 tons) and thirty-six destroyers of a design which led the world until the latter stages of the Great War. The War itself overtook events and none of the propulsion units reached Russia.

2. The German Baltic Fleet was commanded by Gross-Admiral Prinz Heinrich Von Preussen the brother of the Kaiser. It consisted of seven light cruisers, three submarines and eleven destroyer/torpedo boats, all obsolete.

3. Although the Russians captured the German naval codes/secret books when the light cruiser *Magdeburg* ran aground on 26th August. The British Admiralty received a copy of this invaluable material.

4. The Russian Baltic Fleet was also reinforced by five British submarines which were ordered in to disrupt the German's vital iron ore traffic from

Sweden. The Germans had to introduce the convoy system and divert seventy escorts from the North Sea in order to counter the British activities.

5. The Russian Black Sea Fleet comprised five pre-dreadnought battleships, three cruisers, seventeen destroyers and four submarines. Most of this force was obsolete by 1914 standards. In 1915 the first of the new dreadnought battleships (22,000 tons) was commissioned; destined to have a short and inglorious career, the leadship *Imperatritza Ekaterina II* caught fire at her moorings in Sevastopol on 27 October 1916 and had to be scuttled.

6. The Royalist officers were aware of the growing tide of disaffection amongst their crews, but the counter on this occasion, namely to put to sea to take the crews' minds off things, was not available, for in March 1917 the fleet was iced in.

7. The *Aurora* actually fired blank ammunition, but it had the desired effect.

8. Lenin's initial reaction on hearing of the Kronshtadt Mutiny was to order the disbandment and scuttling of the entire fleet but was dissuaded by Trotsky who took over control of the navy.

9. In 1923 the Baltic Fleet had in commission one battleship, five destroyers and six submarines. The Black Sea Fleet consisted of six cruisers and eighteen destroyers.

10. In respect of the Washington Naval Treaty of 1922 the Russians at a subsequent conference of minor naval powers at Rome demanded a battleship tonnage of 490,000 tons. This would have made them second to the United States and Great Britain; they were eventually persuaded to accept 280,000 tons.

11. The force consisted of three battleships, ten destroyers and five submarines. In November 1924 the French ordered the crews ashore; the ships were left to rot and finally sold for scrap in 1937.

12. In 1929 the Soviet Fleet visited foreign ports for the first time. Units of the Baltic Fleet went to Germany and the Black Sea Fleet visited Italy.

13. In January 1931 the Soviet Government published for the first time an official list of its active units: three battleships, two cruisers (all ex-Tzarist), seventeen destroyers, sixteen submarines and ancillary units.

14. Battleships of the Italian-designed *Vittorio Veneto* class were ordered, but of a much greater tonnage and carrying a main armament of 16-inch guns.

15. For example, according to German accounts there were ninety-four Russian submarines stationed with the Baltic Fleet but only twenty-five were operational and none were deployed at the outbreak of war.

16. Including a dozen big destroyers of Italian design and some forty submarines.

17. Twenty-seven destroyers, six cruisers, fifty-one submarines and an obsolete battleship.

18. The Germans moved light forces and submarines by road, river, and canal from the North Sea Bases to Constanza in the Black Sea.

19. Odessa surrended after two hundred days of siege, much of her war material being brought by light craft of the Red Navy.

20. This is particularly the case in Southern Europe where the Germans were able to dominate and command the Western part of the Black Sea with a force of six small submarines and a flotilla of E-boats.

CHAPTER THREE

The Soviet Navy and the Cold War

The advance of the Red Armies into Central Europe in 1945 did in some respects ease the traditional problems of Russian maritime defence. In the Baltic the permanent acquisition of the Karelian Isthmus from the hapless Finns secured the integrity of Leningrad and by the same token improved the viability of Kronshtadt as a naval base. Further to the west the re-absorption of the short-lived Baltic states gave the navy in Baltiysk[1] a deep-water ice-free port and this soon became the headquarters of the Red Navy Baltic Fleet. In addition with Poland and East Germany as compliant client states not only were further naval base facilities made available, but it also ensured that Russia for the first time could exercise total control over the Southern Baltic shoreline. By the same token territorial acquisition and the 'generosity' of her Southern allies secured Russian control over the Western coastline of the Black Sea.

So long as Russian maritime needs dictated a defensive strategy then their position was improved, but any transition to an offensive strategy, either as an end in itself or to counter the naval developments of likely opponents, presented the same insuperable problems as before. The Soviet ability to move into the open seas was fatally inhibited in the Northern waters by the membership of Norway and Denmark to NATO. At the same time any attempt to break out into the North Atlantic from the Arctic bases would present the same problems already encountered by the Germans, with the Iceland–UK Gap and the Denmark Straits proving major obstacles which would have to be overcome. In the South Turkey still controlled the vital narrows of the Dardanelles and almost the whole length of the North Mediterranean coastline guaranteed air superiority for the Western world.[2]

So, although the Russian position had to some extent improved, the maritime flanks were still extremely exposed and for Stalin the Western threat from the sea must have appeared very real. By 1948 the fragile wartime alliance had dissolved into hostile confrontation against maritime powers, which had given an awe-inspiring demonstration of what seapower can really mean. Between 1941–45 they had carried the war to an enemy often thousands of miles from their own metropolitan territories and only thirty years before these same powers had landed troops on Russian territory in support of the forces of counter-revolution during the Civil War. The Marxist prognosis preached that these powers were now bound to turn to attack the Soviet Union. Against such a threat Stalin felt reasonably secure on land, he had deployed his tank divisions deep into Central Europe and there was a comfortable cushion of some 400 miles between these forces and Russian territory. Therefore apart from the American Atomic Bomb the major threat came from the sea.

In the eight years that Stalin ruled Russia after 1945 Soviet naval planning fell into two broad compartments designed to meet the perceived threat from the West. There was first the long-term plan to give Russia a maritime capability which would eventually, and the time-span was probably envisaged as about ten years, be equal to that of the Western maritime powers. This policy meant a naval programme founded on a balanced surface fleet of cruisers, destroyers and submarines protected by a rejuvenated land-based naval air arm; eventually it was planned to make each of the four fleet areas independently secure.[3] In the light of wartime experiences the Russians did acknowledge the passing of the battleships, and indeed they must have secretly been relieved that this mighty capital ship had passed into history, particulary as the Western world had proved its superiority in this field of naval technology and exposed Russian impotency. The largest surface units in the Russian fleet were now to be the 'Sverdlov' class cruisers, displacing 16,000 tons and armed with 6 inch guns. There is some speculation that these cruisers, together with a new class of big destroyers (or destroyer leaders) were intended to provide the screen for carrier task-forces. If this is the case, and there is no hard evidence to show that Stalin saw the aircraft carrier as the new capital ship in the way in which Western navies had, such task-forces would have been many years away. The level of destruction and disruption caused by the Second World War to the Russian economy was such that they were no closer to possessing the capability for such vessels in the early years of the Cold War than they had been in the pre-war period of the negotiations with the United States.

The second component feature of the naval programme was the more urgent need to meet the immediate threat presented by the navies of the Capitalist West. This apparently involved an intelligent and shrewd mixture of the essential 'Mahanist' theories suitably tailored to meet the particular needs of Soviet defence.[4] There was the 'fortress fleet', or the Naval Coastal Defence Service, which comprised coastal artillery and fortifications, naval infantry or marines, in-shore patrol craft such as gunboats and fast motor torpedo boats and shore-based naval aviation. There was also the 'fleet in being' which were task-forces based around the cruisers, destroyers and submarines working in waters which could be covered by naval aviation; forces that would operate in a strategic defensive but tactically offensive role. Russian contingency plans called for the enemy fleets to be attacked from the air while all surface units laid extensive minefields. This would be followed by the surface attack groups and submarines contesting the passage of the invading enemy while the coastal forces provided the last ditch defence along the maritime frontiers.

It is worth noting that at this particular time Stalin did not envisage using his submarines as commerce raiders as the Germans had done in the face of naval supremacy in the two World Wars. This policy would have required a major deployment of submarines in the Northern Fleet areas from where they could have broken out into the Atlantic shipping lanes. Such evidence as is available indicates that there were never more than thirty units deployed in these waters, out of a total submarine force of more than 300. Given the fact that the Germans were never able to maintain more than one third of their submarine strength on station—the remainder were either being refitted or were sailing to and from patrol areas— it is clear that Russian submarines were intended primarily, if not solely, for defensive purposes. Stalin's main concern was the Baltic and Black Sea flanks, for both were like avenues leading directly into the vital areas of the Soviet Union. Once, for example, the Baltic had been secured in a protracted war, Stalin might then have released his submarines into their traditional role, but this would have required Russian control over the exits to the Baltic and the Soviet conquest of Denmark.

By the time that Stalin died, in March 1953, the naval construction programme was well under way. Six out of the twenty-four planned *Sverdlov* cruisers were at sea together with the new destroyer leaders of the *Skoryi* class.[5] The cruiser deficit had been compensated by taking in hand some of the old 1939 hulls of the *Chapayev* class and bringing them into a state of operational readiness. Even so at no time during this period did the Soviet Navy cause any real anxiety in the minds of Western naval strategists who were to continue to plan for the next twenty years, secure in the knowledge that they had a maritime monopoly over the Russians. Instead as the Russian threat loomed large in the early years of the Cold War the Western response was purely military. Alliances were formed which reflected the prospects for a massive land battle, seen in Second World War overtones with a strategic arm having the additional punch of a limited nuclear capability. Events such as the coup d'état in Czechoslovakia and the Berlin Blockade seemed to point the way to future war and the North Atlantic Alliance in its initial phase paid scant regard to the sea. Large numbers of warships in both the American and British navies were either scrapped or mothballed while the new US Carrier *The United States*[7] was cancelled almost immediately after being laid down in April 1949. This in itself was an indication that Soviet naval capability was still seen in terms of their indifferent performance during the Second World War.

The outbreak of the Korean war in June 1950 did produce some changes in Western naval thinking concerning the Soviet threat from the sea. The war itself increased fears in the West about the proximity of conflict in Europe, but also indicated the need to meet what was seen as the Communist threat on a global basis. This, in turn, led to a renaissance of Western naval power particularly as the navies proved invaluable in the Korean conflict. Units of the US Seventh Fleet began operations off the coast of Korea, south of the 38th parallel, as early as the 25 June 1950 and conducted shore bombardments of the advancing Communist forces before the end of the month. Within a short while warships from ten countries, operating under the UN flag, were involved in a blockade of the whole of the Korean coastline. The landings at Inchon in September 1950, while a risky affair which broke all the 'rules' of amphibious operations, demonstrated the superiority and versatility that command of the sea brings to the land battle being waged against a coastal state. The evacuation of UN forces, cut off by the Communist advance from the Hungnam beach-head that winter, also brought home the lessons and advantages to be derived from maritime superiority and control of the seas. By the Armistice in July 1953, the United Nations fleet comprised four battleships, eight cruisers and more than eighty destroyers, which had among their many tasks fired more than four million shells against Communist positions on land. What was even more impressive was the operational role of the sixteen aircraft carriers which had launched more than a quarter of a million separate sorties from their decks in support of the land battle.

The Korean conflict, although a limited war or 'police action' fought ostensibly under the United Nations banner, re-awakened Western apprehensions of the Soviet threat. By 1953 a thorough survey of Russian capabilities by Western forces revealed for the first time the developing threat from the Soviet navy and, by association, exposed the flaws in NATO planning at that time. The alliance itself was reorganized during the course of the Korean War with the creation of a Supreme Allied Commander (Saceur) to co-ordinate the land battle, and the Lisbon Conference in 1952 put in hand a massive re-armament programme destined to balance the Soviet conventional capability in Europe. The new military structure was rounded off by the setting up of two new commands, Atlantic Command, established in America at Norfolk, Virginia in January 1952 and Channel Command, established in Britain at Portsmouth, the following month. The creation of the Atlantic Command (Aclant) was a reflection of Western fears for a struggle for sea communications in which they envisaged a massive onslaught by Soviet submarines. Such a fear at this particular stage was unfounded but nevertheless, awed by the Russian submarine strength, Western navies began to concentrate on their own antisubmarine capabilities, which had been somewhat neglected since 1945. Thus when the Russian submarine threat did really emerge in the late Fifties they had secured a considerable technological lead in this vital area.

Prior to these developments, the American Navy had already moved into the nuclear field when in 1947 a Neptune, at the time the only navy aircraft capable of carrying the still cumbersome atomic bomb, was launched from the *USS Coral Sea*.[8] The US Navy believed that it had a vital role to perform in this field since the B29, the Airforce's strategic bomber was vulnerable to the new Soviet MIG.15 jet interceptors. However, the Airforce, only recently created as an independent arm and jealous of its role, saw the Navy as poaching on its traditional reserve. The *USS United States*, which would have been able to operate a squadron of atomic-armed bombers was cancelled on the slipway as a result of inter-service jealousies. The Korean War brought about a change in Airforce attitudes: it saw the Navy as a complementary arm rather than a competitor and encouraged it to develop a strike capability. The atomic bomb had been reduced in size and weight which made it a proposition for carrier strike aircraft and the new programme went ahead with customary American speed and ingenuity for improvisation. A new twin-engined bomber, the A2 Savage, armed with atomic bombs was operating from specially converted Essex and Midway class carriers by 1956. This involved a strengthened flight deck to carry the additional weight and smaller island super-structures to facilitate handling, while steam catapults launched these heavily laden aircraft from a crowded deck. A new carrier construction programme saw the introduction of the *Forrestal Class* of 60,000 tons,[9] and the revolutionary atomic-powered *USS Enterprise* of 90,000 tons was laid down in 1958 and com-missioned in 1961. Throughout the Fifties when the Cold War reached new peaks of tension and crisis the United States Navy always deployed at least ten large aircraft carriers with a nuclear strike capability. These awesome vessels were organized into Carrier Strike Groups, each with two or three carriers, and were deployed with the Second Fleet in the North Atlantic, the First Fleet in the Central Pacific (based at Pearl Harbour) and the Sixth Fleet in the Mediterranean, with its headquarters in Naples. In 1957 a new fleet was permanently constituted with the Seventh Fleet in South-East Asia operating off the Indo-China coast. As new carriers became available the older *Essex* class were paid off and scrapped. New developments and designs, many of British invention, were incorporated in the new carriers such as mirror-deck landing systems and the angled flight deck. Therefore with the United States Navy playing its part in the Dulles-inspired strategy of massive retaliation it was this sea-borne atomic potential which led to a major revision of Soviet Naval tactics and deployment.

After the death of Stalin the Russian Navy could not help but notice the direction that the Western maritime threat was taking with this heavy and much publicized emphasis on carrier strike.

In the five years up to 1958 Khrushchev saw the Soviet counter to the carrier task groups in the development of submarines as a first line, supported by surface units and aircraft armed with cruise missiles. This in a very real sense reflected a return to the 'Young School of Strategy' of the pre-war days with its heavy emphasis on submarines and light surface forces; the only difference was the substitution of the cruise missile for the torpedo. Khrushchev, in his headstrong and impetuous manner, showed every intention of scrapping the Stalinist programme for a powerful surface fleet: he castigated the navy as 'metal eaters' and favoured any solution which would release vital steel production for other non-military uses. By the same token he was equally anxious to build up the Soviet mercantile marine, which had been sadly neglected for so long and saw shipyard capacity being utilised to meet this pressing need. For Khrushchev the big cruisers and destroyers belonged to an arena of warfare which he regarded as archaic, the protracted conventional war. Instead he sought to concentrate the Soviet defence industries on the deterrent-based strategic nuclear missile. The naval establishment for a few desperate years joined forces with the armoured warfare school in the army to seek a revision of the dictates and influence of the missile enthusiasts in the Kremlin. The cruise missile, which was nothing more than an unmanned bomber, could at this stage of its development be launched only when the submarine was surfaced, and it needed either another ship or aircraft over the horizon to direct it onto its target, for it possessed no organic guidance system. This clearly shows that the Russian strategists envisaged the encounter zone to lie within a few hundred miles of the Russian coast and therefore within range of their own aircraft.

During the vital years between 1953–58 the balance of naval power deteriorated sharply for the Russians and the naval programme instituted to conform to their new strategy proved to be founded on totally the wrong premise: in 1958 the Russians suddenly realized that the Americans possessed a seaborne delivery system which, at a stroke, would make their defence obsolescent. The new American carriers together with the first generations of ballistic missile armed submarines could hit at targets deep inside metropolitan Russia from areas well beyond the range of their own shore-based aviation. The areas of threat for Russia were no longer exclusively confined to the narrow waters of the Baltic and Black Seas but instead extended to an arc stretching from the Eastern

Mediterranean to the Norwegian Sea. In a series of panic decisions the cruise-missile programme was hastily abandoned in favour of shorter-range missiles and a new class of hunter-killer submarines, and at the same time a new emphasis was placed on the neglected techniques of longer range anti-submarine warfare. For the next few years, at least extending into the early Sixties, the Soviet Navy must have been in some disarray.

There is a time-lag of some five years or more between the decision to implement a new strategy and the weapon systems being deployed (particularly at sea) to meet the needs of that strategy. Thus when the re-evaluation was made in 1959 the ships which were being deployed were those which reflected the strategies agreed some five years previously. This explains why the Western world continued to enjoy an assured maritime supremacy over the Soviet navy until the mid-Sixties. Even as the Russians continued to cast apprehensive eyes at the American carrier capability this strike-force was already being replaced by the Polaris submarines as the main instrument of nuclear delivery at sea; this the Russians were not to appreciate for at least another three years.

Ever since the end of the Second World War the United States had been experimenting with a submarine-launched ballistic missile and like the Soviet Union this system was initially based on captured stockpiles of the German V2 rocket. Both powers began to look even more seriously at the project in the early Fifties and although this aspect does represent the one consistent strand in Soviet post-war maritime strategy they soon lost ground to the Americans. The problems presented by such a project were enormous. In the first instance it required a missile with a much longer range than the V2 which could be launched from a submarine which was submerged. It then required that the missile system could be placed in a submarine which was atomic-powered and whose hull allowed for both sustained high speed and a stable launching platform. The Russians, with their inclination for caution and prudence, first tested the nuclear propulsion plants in a surface ship, in this case the icebreaker *Lenin* completed in 1959.[10] The American Navy, supported by the fully mobilised resources of industry and technology, moved directly into the field of atomic-powered submarines. In this type of submarine the heat of a nuclear reactor is transmitted to water, which generates steam and this is used to drive the main propulsion turbines and the turbo-generators. The same power plant is used both above and beneath the surface and this means that the vessel does not have to surface to re-charge its batteries. Nuclear propulsion can generate immense power which can be utilized for high submerged speed provided that the configurations and design of the hull is correct; this raises problems of a similar nature to passing the sonic barrier in the air.

The United States built one submarine to test the nuclear plant which was called the *Nautilus* and a second, conventionally powered ship, the *Albacore*, to test the hull. On the 17 January 1955 the *Nautilus* made the historic signal 'underway on nuclear power.' As a stop-gap measure until the new submarines were available and also to test the needs and problems of launching a missile from beneath the surface, the United States constructed a third experimental submarine. This involved taking two of the new conventionally-powered attack submarines of the Darter class (*USS Growler* and *Grayback*), cutting them in two on the building way and lengthening them by approximately fifty feet. Two cylindrical hangers each eleven feet high and seventy feet long were superimposed on their bows to carry the *Regulus* surface-to-surface cruise missile. The superb organizational infra-structure of the US Navy at this time had enabled them to build a new submarine, decide on its strategic function and organizational role before the missile was even constructed. This in itself must stand out as a most impressive achievement especially when it is compared to the confusion and disarray which characterized the Soviet performance. Then in 1956 the Americans achieved the breakthrough they had been looking for in the field of missile technology. The US Navy had been very apprehensive at the thought of carrying the highly unstable liquid-fuelled missiles in their submarines, and the huge *Jupiter* missile of this type would have required an atomic submarine displacing at least 8,000 tons to carry just a few of these weapons which, even then, could have been launched with the vessel only partially submerged. The development of the solid-fuelled missiles together with the technology of 'miniaturisation' made a ballistic-missile armed submarine a feasible proposition: smaller vessels could now be constructed in which the missile armoury could be quad-rupled. The first Nuclear-Powered Fleet Ballistic Submarine and 'name ship' of its class *USS George Washington*[11] was completed in November 1959 and successfully fired a Polaris Missile in July of the following year.[12] The Polaris AI missile, though solid-fuelled, had a range of less than 1,700 miles which meant that the submarines had to approach fairly close into Soviet Waters before its targets were in range. The Russians were aware that this threat could be countered by anti-submarine forces operating under the protection of shore-based air cover. They were already experimenting with helicopters equipped with homing anti-submarine weapons, but given the speeds of the submarine substantial areas of ocean would have to be covered. This required a larger helicopter platform than could then be carried on the conventional destroyer or even cruiser. A purpose-built helicopter cruiser, the *Moskva*, was laid down at Nikolayev in 1962 and joined the fleet via the Dardenelles in 1968. Once again the time-lag between strategy and construction is revealed for by the time this vessel was completed the American nuclear submarines were equipped with the Polaris A3, a missile system with a range of over 2,500 nautical miles, well beyond any cover provided by shore-based aircraft. It is interesting that on this occasion it was the turn of Western naval analysts to be wrong, for the manner and timing of the entry of the *Moskva* into the Mediterranean, in the aftermath of a Middle East War led them to presume she was intended for amphibious warfare. It was only later when intelligence reports of the small size of her helicopters were appreciated that the *Moskva* was correctly appraised in an anti-submarine context.

As the Cold War moved towards the climactic events of the Cuban Missile Crisis of the early Sixties, the Western navies still felt assured of their maritime superiority over the Soviet Fleet. The Russians, though, did provide a number of surprises in the Sputnik episode in 1957 and this resulted in the false perceptions of a 'missile gap' on the part of the United States. The impact of this was seen as a boost to already existing naval programmes and in particular an emphasis towards more and better armed Nuclear Powered Fleet Ballistic submarines.

Notes

1. In the Gulf of Danzig in what used to be Lithuania.
2. In the Far East, possession of Southern Sakhalin and the Kuril Islands turned the Sea of Okhotsk into an inland sea but the position of the main fleet base at Vladivostock has not altered.
3. For example, the Northern Fleet in the Kola Inlet, the Baltic, the Black Sea and the Pacific in Vladivostock/Petro Pavlovsk.
4. Alfred Thayer Mahan (1840–1914) U.S. naval officer and historian. Became

recognised as an authority on naval strategy and by the turn of the century his writings were exerting a profound influence on seapower in the leading maritime states. He was able to combine a career as naval officer and writer, and during his career published some twenty books of which three are particularly famous: *The Influence of Seapower upon History 1660–1783* (published in 1890); *The Influence of Seapower upon the French Revolution and Empire 1793–1812* (published in 1892); *The Life of Nelson* (published in 1897).

5. Originally there were to be 85 destroyers of this class but only 75 were constructed and of these 20 were transferred to other states. Maximum displacement of 3,500 tons with a main armament of 5.1 inch guns.

6. There were five ships of this class of 15,000 ton cruiser whose design show a marked Italian influence. In 1975 two ships remain in service as training cruisers.

7. CVA58.

8. CVA43: 52,000 ton Attack Carrier.

9. '*Forrestal*' class of six ships, the lead ship laid down in July 1952 was completed in October 1955.

10. The *Lenin* was the world's first nuclear-powered surface ship to put to sea.

11. There were five submarines of the class displacing 1,700 tons submerged.

12. Prior to this in the 1957 Fiscal Year Program provision was made for 4 *Skate* class nuclear-powered attack submarines (SSN). The same ship became famous in the early Sixties for the record-breaking underwater endurance cruises.

CHAPTER FOUR

The Cuban Missile Crisis

For the student of international relations the Cuban missile crisis provides a striking illustration of the use of coercion, both through the annunciation of threats and the subtle use of maritime power as a delicate instrument of foreign policy, without actually crossing the threshold of violence. Given the direct nature of the physical confrontation and the pressures influencing the decisions reached by the chief protagonists, the impact of restraints on the actual use of violence stands out as quite remarkable.

The type and quality of government operating in Cuba has constantly posed for the United States the dilemma of its relations with the neighbouring states of Central America and the Caribbean. It can either accept the government as being the legitimate source of power, authority and the means through which it should conduct Cuban-American relations, no matter how disreputable that government may be, or it can seek to remove the offending government and replace it with another. Both forms of action provide major problems for any American administration. In the first case a hostile government can prevent a normal relationship and this could be disastrous, for Cuba lies only ninety miles from Florida in an area of vital importance to the military security of the United States. On the other hand, to seek to remove that government violates one of the fundamental principles of international relations, non-intervention, and short of an acquisitive policy there is no means of ensuring that the new government would prove to be any more amenable to the United States than its predecessor. American interests built up over more than half a century of relations with Cuba extended beyond the questions of defence

40

and security. The United States had possession of a naval base at Guantanamo Bay and American interests infiltrated into practically every branch of the economy: banks, railways, electricity, telephones and even the sugar industry were almost all entirely in American hands. Despite the brutality and flagrant corruption of the Batista régime the United States steadfastly supported it with arms and money against the revolutionary forces led by Fidel Castro, from 1952 until its collapse in 1959. Castro preached social revolution and to the inflexible American mind of the late Fifties this could only mean Communism. Cuban-American relations deteriorated with the Americans embarking on a form of economic warfare and Castro responding by appropriating American property and investments on the island.[1] In April 1960 some 1,500 Cuban exiles, trained and equipped in Florida and Guatemala by the Central Intelligence Agency, landed at Playa Giron in the Bay of Pigs. This invasion attempt was a complete disaster and the Kennedy Administration could not deny that it was heavily implicated in the venture.

For the Russians, Cuba after the Castro Revolution was seen as the Soviet gateway to Latin America, for it was hoped that the Cuban revolution would spark off popular movements and instabilities on a continent that had remained a reliable supporter to the United States since the early nineteenth century. Guatemala had tried after a left-wing coup in 1954 to secure Soviet arms and support, but this movement had been killed by an American sponsored counter-revolution. Khrushchev turned to Cuba where he hoped to demonstrate his skills in diplomacy and help silence the swelling ranks of his critics at home. It was hardly surprising that links between the two states were formally acknowledged when Raul Castro, the brother of Fidel, headed a diplomatic mission to Moscow in July 1960. In the same month the Kremlin, which had already led the voices of protest in condemning the Bay of Pigs as 'bullying imperialism' on the part of the United States, became a little more explicit in its attitudes, when Khrushchev in a major speech said:

'Figuratively speaking, Soviet artillerists can, in case of necessity, support the Cuban people by rocket fire if the aggressive forces of the Pentagon should dare to start an intervention against Cuba.'[2]

The failure of the Bay of Pigs operation did not in any way lessen American sensitivity over Castro's Cuba and this was reflected in the Congressional Elections of 1962 which saw a powerful and vociferous Republican demand on Kennedy to take a harder line against Khrushchev's 'brinkmanship' and Castro's Communist government. The Berlin crisis[3] the previous year had left an air of uncertainty in the relations between the super powers as they now moved towards a major clash of their global interests.

The Soviet Union was, by 1962, genuinely alarmed by what had become the 'missile gap' in reverse. When statistics of comparative nuclear strengths were made public in 1962 they showed that not only did the United States have a vastly superior first strike capability but that their second strike capability was as great as that for a Soviet first strike. Khrushchev disturbed by the McNamara strategy of counter-force[4] saw the need to diversify Russia's strategic forces as a stop-gap measure until nuclear parity could be attained. One way around this problem was to deploy Soviet medium-range missiles (MRBMs) within range of the United States. Cuba seemed ideal and so this Caribbean outpost simultaneously became the focus of American sensitivity and a temporary Soviet solution to restore the strategic balance in their favour.

In the summer of 1962 reports began to reach the United States of a major Soviet arms build-up on the island. These reports brought in mostly by Cuban exiles, talked initially only of conventional weapons, but Kennedy in early September approved an order that the entire island should be kept under photographic surveillance. On the 28th September reconnaissance photographs of a Soviet freighter en route for Cuba showed a deck cargo which intelligence analysts determined were the fuselages of the Ilyushin 28 bomber, a medium-range tactical aircraft capable of carrying a nuclear payload. It was not until late evening on Monday 15th October that hard evidence in the form of air photographs gave defence analysts incontrovertible proof that installations for offensive missiles were being constructed in Cuba. Throughout that night they checked and re-checked the evidence, informed their own chiefs who, following the recognized procedure, reported to McGeorge Bundy, Kennedy's special adviser on National Security Affairs. The President himself was informed the next morning and by noon the group, later to be known as the Executive Committee of the National Security Council, had assembled in the Cabinet room. It seemed clear to everyone that the Soviet Union had hoped to complete the installation of the missiles in Cuba in secrecy so that the unveiling of these missiles when they were operational would take the form of a *fait accompli* to which the United States would be unable to find a satisfactory non-violent response.

This exclusive Council of War with which the President was to surround himself for the next fifteen days saw further and even more sinister motives behind the Soviet move. Although Western commentators have since doubted whether the Soviet decision involved anything more than an attempt to resolve the nuclear balance, there is no escaping the fact that the United States was presented with a nasty set of alternatives. If the Americans did nothing then their alliances could be fatally undermined; large question marks would be raised against the integrity of the American commitment to defend its partners. Thus if Khrushchev made another play for Berlin the Western position could have become untenable even before the crisis began. On the other hand, if the Americans took the missiles out through some form of direct military action it could leave them wide open as a target for propaganda and condemnation, as well as inviting a Russian counter over Berlin.[5] There was an awareness right from the very beginning that any United States response might worsen the world situation. But not challenging the Soviet move would surely be the worst course of all. During the next few days the objective was decided, to remove the strategic missiles from Cuba, and with this clear the advisers sought to provide the President with the range of options open to him. The Kennedy response was to combine a naval 'blockade'[6] with a very strong public warning to the Soviet Union of the risks of reprisal against herself if the missiles deployed in Cuba were used against the United States. That initial week of secrecy had been absolutely necessary not only because of the American need to work out carefully a co-ordinated plan, but also because they feared that the Russians might over-react if they learned that their plans were known. At seven p.m. on Monday 22nd October, President Kennedy made a broadcast on radio and television in which he revealed the nature of the Soviet moves on Cuba and the naval quarantine. The crux of his message came in a tersely worded warning to the Soviet Union:

It shall be the policy of this nation to regard any nuclear missile launched from Cuba against any nation to the Western hemisphere as an attack by the Soviet Union on the United States, requiring a full retaliatory response upon the Soviet Union.[7]

During the first week of the crisis when the exclusive Council of War was at work in preparing the options, the need to avoid violence was recognized as of paramount importance. It is hardly surprising therefore that the United States should choose 'blockade' of Cuba as their initiatory response rather than an airstrike or an invasion. The blockade avoided the risk of killing Russians and reflected the American desire not to initiate violence. Besides escalating the crisis, overt violence would have invited world criticism. Instead, the United States sought, in the arena of the Atlantic and the Caribbean, to manipulate the risk of violence and place the onus squarely on the Russians.

The crisis held, from the outset, the serious potential danger of incidents occuring which in themselves could have led to inadvertent hostilities and even unmanageable escalation. The physical setting of the confrontation at sea made it inevitable that individual captains would, by the very force of events, have a larger degree of operational control over the specific points of contact. This was succinctly expressed by Henry Pachter when he wrote:

> 'If any sea captain had a loose hand on the trigger, naval war might break out.'[8]

So although the American decision did raise the spectre of a tense and delicate situation at sea it had the obvious advantage of making a clear challenge to the Soviet move and it presented Khrushchev with uneasy and very unattractive alternatives.[9] Russia could avoid a collision at sea, but if there was to be violence Khrushchev would be clearly cast in the role of the instigator, and with world opinion at stake this was in itself a vital consideration.

There were a number of ways in which the Russians could treat the blockade, the most obvious and violent would have been to break it either with submarines or surface vessels. Secondly, they could convoy their ships through thereby inviting the Americans to stop them, or simply inform those vessels en route for Cuba to ignore the American navy. Any one of these moves raises the intriguing question of what would have happened had a Soviet merchantman refused to stop when ordered to do so by an American warship. There were a number of options open to the Americans but all involved violence. They could have deployed sufficient warships to have physically blocked all five navigable channels that led from the Atlantic to the Caribbean, or steel cables could have been extended between two warships to trap an approaching ship, or there were various devices, such as small-scale depth charges, which could have been dropped to disable the rudders. All of these were discussed by the American navy although which they would have used, had the need arisen, has never been publically revealed.

The blockade, or quarantine line, was manned from October 24th when it was known that there were twenty-five merchant ships en route for Cuba from the Soviet Union. The line patrolled by the American warships was only 500 miles from Cuba which put the ships within range of the Soviet MIG 21's on their Cuban airfields, but it had the essential advantage of allowing the Soviet leader enough time to reach an 'unhurried decision' before the first Russian ship arrived in the encounter zone. Throughout that first day no Soviet ship reached the quarantine line and that evening it was reliably reported that twelve Russian ships had altered course (presumably those which had the incriminating cargoes). At eight in the morning of Wednesday 25th October the first Soviet ship was challenged. This vessel was an oil tanker called the *Bucharest* and she was allowed to sail on without being boarded. The Americans could afford to show restraint, to make a gesture and at the same time not take any action which could undermine the credibility of the blockade. The incident of the *Bucharest* does reveal the subtleties of the diplomatic game being played out on the high seas, for by asking the tanker to identify itself the Americans had 'established' the blockade, but by not boarding the ship had allowed the Russians to claim that there had been no interference with its ships in international waters. The first boarding occurred on the morning of Friday 26th October. Throughout the previous night two destroyers had been shadowing a freighter; at eight in the morning she was ordered to stop and a party of seamen was put aboard. This vessel the *Maruda* was registered in the Lebanon, manned by a Greek crew, and under charter to the Russian Government, so therefore not, in international law, a Russian ship. When the search revealed no cargo which contravened the terms of the quarantine, she was allowed to proceed to Cuba.

These incidents covering the first four days of the crisis show that Khrushchev was in effect 'ignoring' the naval response since he sought to regain the' initiative without breaking the blockade: the Russians concentrated their attention on bringing to operational deployment their missiles already in Cuba with the resources, material and back-up systems on the island. As far as the blockade was concerned Khrushchev seemed content to declare publicly, but cautiously, that the American action was illegal, although in private conversations in Moscow with William Knox, an American industrialist, he did adopt a more bellicose manner.[10] Yet the naval operations at sea did exert a strange and at the same time terrifying influence over events. The Americans in particular recognized that once Kennedy had made public the issue of the missiles in Cuba time was of the utmost importance, so that a non-violent solution could be found before the violent solutions became predominant.

Kennedy had recently read a book by Barbara Tuchman,[11] called *The Guns of August*, a new definitive account relating the events leading up to the outbreak of the Great War. The theme of this work was that once a course of action has begun the events are taken over by a sense of 'built-in logic' which gives to past actions in the sequence a strong influence on decisions about the future. The influence of this feature of international relations, which is frequently referred to as 'the Crisis Slide', was not lost on Kennedy, who at times felt on the brink of disaster and maybe losing control of events which had begun with his broadcast and the implementation of the blockade. Khrushchev must have been thinking along similar lines, as is clearly revealed by both the tone and substance of his statement to the Supreme Soviet on 12 December 1962, one phrase of which is particularly revealing:

'the fuse of war which had already been lighted'.

The Soviet response of avoiding a collision course on the blockade while working to complete the missile deployment with resources on hand forced the Americans to escalate the crisis even further. By Friday 26th October the exchange of notes between the White House and the Kremlin had sought only to confuse the situation. The United Nations Secretary General U Thant tried to take the sting out of the crisis but both sides seemed still on a collision course. The action of the Russians to continue the missile site construction forced the Americans to contemplate other forms of response. The late editions of many of that evening's newspapers had headlines on possible invasion or bombing. At the White House officials told reporters that the choice was between expansion of the blockade and some form of air action. Along the Southern shores of the United States naval units were deployed to support troop landings and airborne formations were placed on readiness to parachute into Cuba and seize the sites. Throughout the crisis the airforce continually flew over the island and had the Russians not backed down perhaps the world would have witnessed the physical execution of the newly defined McNamara Strategy of Flexible Response.[12] Later that same evening a note was received from the Kremlin which at least offered the prospects of a negotiated settlement. Although it was long, rambling, and even ambiguous it did allow the President to extract from it enough to reply with an offer of peace, which contained terms satisfactory to both sides. We still do not know what were the precise influences which forced Khrushchev to accede to American demands but at least it does seem clear that the naval blockade in itself was not the prime force in persuading the Russians to agree to remove their offensive weapons from Cuba; rather the threat of airstrike or invasion seems to have been the crucial element.

On Saturday 27th October, while the Americans awaited the Soviet reply and the crisis was at its most delicate stage, a couple of incidents occurred which threatened to escalate the confrontation over the threshold to violence. The need to control events had led the Americans to exercise extreme caution in other areas of confrontation with the Soviet Union. Kennedy had personally ordered the U2 reconnaissance flights not to stray into Soviet territory in case they were mistaken on early warning radar as an incoming atomic bomber force. That morning a U2 strayed into Soviet airspace over the Chutotsk Peninsular in the Northern Arctic regions. Immediately American fighters were scrambled from their Alaskan bases with orders to search for the missing spy plane and escort it back to safety. Soviet intercepters based on Wrangel Island scrambled to intercept the intruder, but the Americans found their errant comrade first and the Soviets allowed the incident to pass. In the South however the U2 flights over Cuba had continued unabated throughout the crisis and had been augmented by special low-level reconnaissance missions flown by Navy Neptunes. Fidel Castro who had been shouting defiance on Cuban television and issuing threats to shoot down these intruders, finally kept his promise: a U2 was destroyed and another damaged by anti-aircraft fire. Had Castro acted alone? or had the Russians ordered the shooting? At this delicate stage of the game the Americans wisely decided not to retaliate. But there was no mistaking the mood when the Pentagon warned that it would resist any interference with its reconnaissance flights and underlined this by calling up another 14,000 air reservists. Contingency plans to destroy the Cuban anti-aircraft sites were put into an advanced state of readiness and had they become operative it is difficult to see how casualties to both Cuban civilians and Russian 'technicians' could have been avoided. In such an event it is possible that the crisis would have moved beyond any point where it could have been controlled and large-scale fighting could have ensued. The Americans felt reasonably sure that it would not go nuclear, but they did feel that conventional conflict in Cuba might provoke Moscow into counter-action elsewhere. However, it does need to be stressed that whereas the Pentagon could feel confident in the overall American nuclear superiority this would have been of little comfort if Russian perceptions were different and they in turn initiated a nuclear exchange that neither side could win.

On Sunday morning Moscow radio announced that the Soviet Premier had ordered, in return for American guarantees to recognize the integrity of Cuban sovereignty, that all work should be stopped on the missile sites and that the weapons should be returned to the Soviet Union. At noon while a diplomatic note was being despatched over the wires to the Kremlin, an official statement was broadcast praising Premier Khrushchev's 'statesman-like decision' in what was seen as a 'welcome and constructive contribution to peace.[13]

There is a widely-held journalistic myth which sees the Cuban crisis as one of the climactic events in the whole post-war period. The crisis did act as a catalyst, for it induced changes in the long-standing patterns of international politics. The actual confrontation was geographically very limited although its outcome had world-wide implications and consequences. In the first instance this was because the confrontation powers infused into the area of the crisis a symbolic significance for a broader spectrum of world politics. Secondly the stratagems involved in the dispute undermined the hitherto clearly demarcated lines of political control and spheres of political influence.

The United States had mobilised an awe-inspiring array of conventional forces and were determined to ensure their control of an area of the world which they considered to be vital to their own security. At sea the American navy performed its task with skill and efficiency which stands in stark contrast to the Soviet performance. Those Russian ships that did cross the quarantine line were obviously under the strictest orders to be extremely co-operative in submitting to any search. There were six Soviet submarines in the Caribbean–Atlantic region during the crisis and they were all monitored and tracked continuously by American warships. The submarines were conventional diesel-powered vessels who could do little to escape surveillance or intervene in the crisis.

It has become fashionable to date the emergence of a modern Soviet navy from the rebuff and rough handling it experienced at the time of Cuba. Western awareness of a new direction and shift in emphasis in Soviet deployments only became widespread in 1964 and it was natural to see this in terms of the Cuban crisis. However, the role and function of Soviet seapower in the sixties which is discussed more fully in the next chapter was a result of decisions taken and plans made in the late fiftees and any relation to Cuba is purely coincidental. What Cuba did reveal to the Russians was the need for an all-nuclear submarine fleet, in terms of both missile boats and the traditional hunter-killer. It revealed American naval superiority and reflected the need for the Russians to concentrate on the strategic defence over their own waters. Finally it encouraged the Soviet Admirals to speak out against such adventurist policies of supporting sympathetic states so far from Soviet Russia. The decision to relinquish any interest in the Indonesian Navy and instead to concentrate on the naval forces of countries nearer home like Egypt and Algeria seems to underline this new tenet of Soviet maritime doctrine.

Notes

1. By the end of 1960 US investments in Cuba, amounting to approximately 1,000,000,000 dollars, had been seized.

2. Speech made 9th July 1960. Reported in *Pravda* 10 July 1960.

3. The events leading up to the Berlin Wall August 1961.

4. The basic assumption of a counter-force strategy is that war, even nuclear war is a real contingency that has to be recognized. Therefore if war breaks out the country's first and foremost preoccupation should be to limit damage from enemy strikes. That can only be achieved by hitting the enemy's strategic bases—airfields and missile sites—as a first step, as early as possible in war. As the other side is also likely to have the same type of force, the war will be a contest of 'long-range artillery duel'.

5. It is important to point out that the State Department firmly believed at this time that the construction of the Berlin Wall was but the first part of some grand and sinister Soviet strategy.

6. Technically the United States quarantined Cuba since 'blockade' is an incident of war.

7. The full text of Kennedy's speech is in *The Cuban Crisis of 1962. Selected Documents and Chronology*, ed. David L. Laron (Boston, Houghton, Mifflin 1963) pp. 41–46.

8. Henry Pachter, *Collision Course*, (New York: Praeger, 1963) p. 42.

9. The Russians had already been trying to alleviate American sensitivities over Cuba by pointing out that they had no need to deploy nuclear missiles into Cuba. A TASS communique of 11th September stated:

    'Our nuclear weapons are so powerful in their explosive force and the Soviet Union has rockets so powerful to carry these nuclear war heads that there is no need to search for sites for them beyond the boundaries of the Soviet Union.'

    The full text of this communique is in Pachter, *Collision Course*, p. 177.

10. Secret unofficial discussions between an American reporter and a Soviet agent are reported to have been a vital channel of communication between Kennedy and Khrushchev. A more detailed account of this intriguing aspect can be found in 'The Cuban Crisis: How Close We Were to War', *Look*, 25 August 1964, pp. 17–21.

11. In Britain it was published as *August 1914* (London: Constable, 1962).

12. The general thrust of the Kennedy Administration's military strategy was the emphasis on the doctrines of flexible response and multiple options: the creation of a military force which would remain under tight civilian control at all times and which would be used in a variety of ways to meet a variety of threats. For a more detailed account see William W. Kaufman, *The MacNamara Strategy* (New York: Harper and Row, 1964).

13. See the London *Times*, Monday 29 October 1962.

CHAPTER FIVE

The Emergence of the Modern Soviet Navy

At the time of Cuba and for a short while afterwards American carrier strength reached its zenith[1] and thus presented the Soviet defence planners with a host of new and complex problems. So long as the prime American threat had been perceived in the form of manned bombers then the Soviet counter was a fairly straightforward proposition. The American planes operated from bases in Spain, North Africa and the islands of the West Pacific ocean.[2] The distances to the Soviet Union from the bomber fields, the high altitude approaches, and especially the known base locations facilitated Soviet defence plans. However, the appearance of the new carrier groups operating in the Western Pacific, North Atlantic and Mediterranean changed the picture completely. The new super carriers, such as *Forrestal* and *Enterprise*, carried the supersonic Vigilante strike aircraft with a speed of Mach 2.0 (I.E. 1400 m.p.h.) and a range of more than 3,000 miles.[3] The carrier group was protected by an air defence system built around the then new and redoubtable multi-purpose Phantom, while cruisers provided missile defence with the Talos[4] which could give cover up to a distance of fifty miles.

The initial Soviet response to counter the carrier strike threat was given an exceedingly high priority even at the expense, in terms of ship-building programmes, of the Soviet submarine-borne nuclear delivery system. Thus a base for hunter-killer submarines was established in Albania[5] to watch US VIth Fleet Activities in the Mediterranean. The *Kynda* class cruiser programme was cancelled and only four out of the projected twelve were completed; the vacated slipways were then used to boost the *Kashin* class, as an interim destroyer. Secondly, the development programme for a long-range surface-to-surface missile (SSM) as an anti-carrier weapon was accelerated. Valuable time and wasted effort was spent in the futile construction of such weapons, even though it must be assumed that Soviet strategists and technologists must have been aware of the inherent weaknesses and drawbacks of such a system. Any missile which has a range of over twenty-five miles— i.e. beyond the horizon—must have an aircraft, or surface vessel, to co-ordinate the attack and guide the weapon onto its final target. The technology for such a function is incredibly complex in itself and in terms of operational strategy was by all the normal laws of war a non-starter. It would have required a long-range Soviet aircraft to operate in airspace dominated by the carrier's own supersonic interceptors. In addition there are problems connected with the missile itself: it is large, cumbersome and when mounted on the relatively small Soviet hulls creates a whole series of problems in terms of stowage and handling facilities. Finally, a new class of Soviet submarine was laid down to counter the carrier. This was the *Echo* class nuclear-powered attack vessel equipped with the Shaddock cruise missile; the first one appeared in 1962.

The American debate over the role of the carrier strike threat provides one of the great ironies in the tale of the Soviet navy, for their monopoly of attention as an integral part of the Western armoury did not survive the Kennedy era. Their role in the nuclear battle order was first seriously questioned by Western strategists and within a very short while they were down-graded in favour of the new and improved Polaris submarines and land-based Intercontinental Ballistic Missiles (ICBMs). Despite the technical excellence of the carrier strike group,[6] a surface force of this description was still seen as desperately vulnerable. A tactical cruise missile fired by an *Echo* submarine was a nuclear weapon, the *Kashin* class destroyers also had Shaddocks, while TU16 *Badger* bomber was armed with a stand-off nuclear bomb.[7] Against threats of this description all-round defence had to be absolutely certain. The image of a nuclear air-burst above a carrier group was a spectre which increasingly haunted American strategists, and against which, of course, no weapon system could be devised to ensure total defence. Even more fundamental was the role which the carrier force would be required to fulfil in a conflict situation. It had been originally envisaged as a force that would bombard Soviet naval bases and targets close in to the coastline in a 'broken-backed' war. But given the increasingly destructive capability of the ICBMs and the accompanying Polaris force a 'broken-backed' type of war on the lines of the early Forties became a very unlikely contingency.

The American questioning of the carrier role coincided with the beginning of what was later to be known as the 'great carrier debate' in the United Kingdom. The British, as the inventors of the aircraft carrier, now embarked upon a period of quite bitter controversy,[8] which was to lead to the decision to withdraw the carrier in its traditional form from the Fleet. The circumstances were different, however, since the Royal Navy did not envisage its carriers in the same way as their American counterpart. There were never enough carriers to form a task-force and their aircraft were not capable of a nuclear-strike task. Instead the Royal Navy pinned its faith on an East of Suez commitment in a limited war environment. With the demise of the East of Suez role, the carriers in their traditional form as an integral component of the Fleet, faded from the scene.

Thus while the Soviet Union was attempting to cut the corners to produce a viable counter against what it envisaged as the primary offensive weapon in the American Armoury, the Americans were turning to the Polaris vessels for the 'first division' of their seaborne delivery force. By the time the Russians had come to recognize the shift in American emphasis much valuable time had been lost. The need to shift to new priorities to meet the American threat caused yet more confusion and dismay throughout the whole of the Soviet ship construction industry. By 1962 the US nuclear submarine programme was flourishing with twenty-seven vessels in commission. Nine were Polaris submarines and the remainder were attack submarines, the hunter-killers. However, what was even more impressive was the number of submarines under construction. Eleven high speed attack and nineteen Polaris were on the way and more were being planned.

To understand the Soviet reaction to the new menace posed by Polaris it is necessary to appreciate the impact that such force lends to the overall nuclear balance. Soviet military doctrine sees nuclear deterrence and general concepts of defence as being synonymous. Thus a total nuclear war would involve calculations over nuclear exchange in which the Soviet Union having first thrown back a Western attack would then, in their eyes, go on to win. In the last resort the Soviet Union even saw a partially damaged zone in Europe as the area to rebuild the Socialist system once the two metropolitan territories had been destroyed. Thus the Russians believed that if war was forced on them by the United States it need not be mutual suicide. However, the development of the American Polaris system completely upset the Soviet calculations. These missiles could not be countered (except in the grand strategic sense by their own kind) and neither could they be detected. To the Russians they were seen as bestowing upon the United States the awful advantage of strategic flexibility, for they could be introduced into the nuclear exchange at any stage and thus deny the Soviet Union even the hopes of a European haven.

By the time of Cuba the Soviet Union had already taken the decisions that would see the pattern and development of the Soviet navy for some years to come. In principle, the Russian had decided on a strategy of forward defence, but the means by which this could be undertaken were destined to take at least another two years before they were resolved. The Soviet leader, Khrushchev, and his chief adviser on defence, Marshal Zhukov, had displayed no real understanding of what the naval threat, posed by the United States, meant in naval terms. However, the head of the navy, Admiral Gorshkov,[9] although a faithful partyman, was able to come into his own after years in the barren wilderness. Ever since his appointment he had fought carefully and in a cunning way to ensure the survival of the cruiser force as the nucleus of a powerful surface force. The role that he saw such ships fulfilling was to sweep the narrow sea exits (i.e. the Denmark Straits, and Iceland–UK gap) clear of Western anti-submarine vessels so that Soviet submarines could get out to counter the Western forces. It required little refinement to enhance that Soviet task with an anti-submarine role to give the Soviet navy, probably for the first time ever, a realistic, high priority task in the defence of their homeland.

The problem that confronted Gorshkov and his planners was to devise a means by which the Americans would be denied the option of using their Polaris weapons at the *moment* of their choice, and this required that the Soviet navy should destroy the American nuclear submarines in the initial phase of a conflict. In turn Soviet warships would need to control those waters which the Polaris submarines would have to use in order to unleash their missiles on the Soviet Union. The Russians took the range of the Polaris A2 missile as 1500 nautical miles and then drew an arc centred on Moscow. The seas which were contained inside this line were the Eastern Mediterranean Basin and the Norwegian Sea. The first Soviet exercise in keeping with these calculations was reported in the Western press in 1961 when a number of Soviet vessels appeared in the Norwegian Sea. Over the following years this activity built up with a stronger bias in the direction of anti-submarine warfare (ASW) and frequent reinforcements between the main fleet anchorages in the Baltic and the Kola Inlet. By 1964 Soviet vessels were observed on exercise in the Denmark Straits and an increasing number of submarines were seen in the Atlantic approaches.

In order to meet the needs of this limited forward deployment the Soviet Union had at first to adapt what was available: in terms of cruisers there was the *Kynda* class; the first of these ships appeared in 1962. Essentially we would describe the *Kynda* as 'ship killers', displacing less than 6,000 tons and although smaller than many Western destroyers they carry an enormous armament. The main 'battery' is the Shaddock with all its inherent problems,[10] and in addition there is an array of anti-aircraft missiles (SAMs), ASW mortars and torpedoes, and a gun armament of 76 mm calibre which out-ranged its Western equivalents.

The first generation of *Kresta* (I's) appeared in the mid-sixties. This was a larger vessel with an increased displacement (6,500 tons), a reduced Shaddock battery but extra SAMs and a more sophisticated electronics system. Apparently during construction the characteristics were altered to allow for a helicopter hangar and flight-deck aft. This was intended to improve the ASW capability as well as to direct the fire of the missile system.

In terms of destroyers the first of the *Kashin* class appeared at about the same time as the *Kynda* class cruisers. Their particular claim to fame was that they were the first class of ships equipped with all gas turbines, which have the advantage of a cold start, rapid acceleration and a sustained high speed of at least thirty-six knots in clement conditions. Nevertheless these handsome and quite distinctive-looking vessels were a botched solution to a pressing gap in naval requirements. From the outset they were armed with a dated SAM system, and no surface missile capability, helicopters, or variable depth sonar. Within a short period they became out-dated and have recently been relegated to the task of goodwill visits to foreign ports.[11]

In submarine construction the Soviet Union stressed two main priorities. In the first instance a major emphasis was placed on the Soviet version of the Polaris submarine. If the aim was to create a situation of nuclear parity the Russians were destined for more shocks and setbacks. Their vessel given the NATO designation *Yankee* class first appeared in 1967. Its design characteristics owe, apparently, much to a child's plastic construction kit which had appeared in the United States some three years previously. The *Yankee* had sixteen tubes carrying liquid-fuelled rockets with a range of some 1,300 nautical miles. Their nearest equivalent in the US Navy was the *Ethan Allen* SSBNS[12] but even then they were markedly inferior. Nevertheless the Soviet Union stepped up their annual production from eight to ten and by the early Seventies had some twenty-five units operational. Although the range of their missiles was considerably less than the American ships this, from a Russian viewpoint, is more than compensated by the lucrative targets that dwell very close to the Atlantic seaboard. In support of the *Yankee* class older *Hotel* class nuclear vessels and *Golf* class diesel submarines, both armed with the Serb missile,[13] were kept in service.

The other priority in Soviet submarine construction lay in hunter-killers, of which the Russians accord pride of place to the *Charlie* class. They were probably ordered at the same time as the *Yankee* class and are nuclear-powered, but armed with a new generation of cruise missiles. By all accounts the S-SN-7 when it appeared in 1969 represented a new dimension in naval warfare: it can be launched from beneath the surface and has a range, at supersonic speed, of some thirty nautical miles.[14] In addition, two other classes of nuclear-powered hunter-killers appeared during this initial period of Soviet forward deployment. Conventionally armed with torpedo rather than cruise missile they were the *November* and *Victor* classes; the former rejoice under the reputation of 'widow makers' in the Soviet navy. The *November* class are very noisy ships and have suffered from inherent design faults particularly in the shield to the nuclear reactors. It was a vessel of this class that so dramatically (and from a Soviet viewpoint embarrassingly) foundered South-West of the United Kingdom in 1970.

Of all the Soviet warships that made an appearance in the 1960's the one that attracted the greatest and invariably the most hysterical and ill-informed comment from the Western media was the *Moskva*. There is even today some mystery surrounding the origin of these fine 20,000 ton carriers.[15] Some would argue that this first Soviet venture into seaborne aviation was started from scratch whilst others claim that the hulls belong to the cruisers of the *Stalingrad* class which had been discarded and cancelled on the slipway in 1954. In keeping with the traditional trends of Soviet naval design these vessels were intended as test-beds for a much larger carrier which would be constructed at a later date. The *Moskva* represents a hybrid design: the front part resembles a large missile cruiser with the standard fit and range of missilry while the stern portion provides a large and spacious flight deck. The role of the *Moskva* is obviously to operate further out to sea as a command ship for major anti-submarine operations and, with twenty ASW helicopters, is admirably suited to this task. Thus in conceptual terms the *Moskva* represents nothing which is new to Western experience, being a derivation of the converted merchant ships and 'Jeep carriers' operated by the British and Americans in the ASW role in the Atlantic during the Second World War. Presumably the *Moskva* could easily adapt to an amphibious task giving naval infantry heliborne and sea lift over a fairly short distance. Likewise the British and Americans have long since developed the amphibious carrier (commando carriers in the Royal Navy) though unlike their Soviet counterpart the Western ships have always been indifferently armed.

Thus by the mid-Sixties the Naval High Command had been given a number of missions in its 'Defence of the Homeland'. The first task was to counter the Polaris threat, which required hunter-killer submarines and ASW task-forces operating in a forward zone of deployment. The Russian emphasis, in the light of experience in the Caribbean, on nuclear-powered hunter-killers is now regarded by Western analysts as a mistake. In this task the submarine is seen as the weapon which combines stealth with surprise. Except for transit to patrol areas the virtues of speed which nuclear power gives to a submarine is not seen as of any real advantage, especially when balanced against the fact that nuclear power is very noisy underwater. The continued British emphasis on conventional power using electric motors when submerged has resulted, after years of perseverance, in some of the quietest submarines in the world.[16]

The second mission of the Soviet navy was to neutralize the Western Strike Fleet Carriers before they could launch their nuclear-armed aircraft on the Soviet Union. This, as we have seen, involves a combination of weapons but to the forefront were the cruise missile submarines of the *Charlie* class and the long-range aircraft with stand-off bombs of Soviet naval air arm. Thirdly the Soviet

Navy was required to contribute to the Russians' strategic delivery capability. The heavy emphasis on submarines in the Soviet Fleet and the development of particular vessels for specific tasks placed an enormous strain on shipyard construction. In order to cope with the competing priorities it is generally accepted in the West that the proportion of submarine building was:

2 *Charlie* (SSGN) cruise missile-armed submarines: anti-carrier.
3 *Victor* (SSN) fleet submarines purely torpedo-armed: anti-Polaris.
6 *Yankee* (SSBN) Ballistic missile ships.

The other missions allotted to the Navy are self-explanatory, to gain and maintain control of the 'Four Fleet Areas' and especially the avenues of approach in the Baltic, Black and Barents Sea. Finally, the Navy had to provide flank support for land operations along the coastal areas of these waters and therefore fulfill the traditional role of servants to the Army in a general war situation. To discharge these missions there were, of course, a host of Soviet escort vessels, missile patrol boats and a developing capability in landing crafts and amphibious warfare.[17] Many of the older submarines relegated from the primary tasks in the high seas were destined to serve out their days in the coastal formations.[18]

It is particularly noteworthy that attack on maritime lines of communication does not appear on the list of Soviet naval missions. This is an important departure since commerce raiding had hitherto been central to any discussion on the role of the navy and the submarine in particular. It was the Soviet belief at this time that the tasks listed above would be discharged in the environment of a General War and in particular in the initial phases. There were very few submarines, and no modern vessels, which were surplus to requirements to be sent out in 'wolf packs' on the lines of German U-Boats of twenty years before. However, all submarines, and this would include the Ballistic missile boats, are armed with torpedos (as are Western vessels) for use against targets of opportunity that might appear in the appropriate stages of a wartime patrol.

In the period after 1968 the Soviet Navy, in response to the Polaris A3 strategic missile, which had a range of 2,500 nautical miles, extended its forward deployment. This new arc embraced more distant waters new to Soviet warships such as the Arabian Sea, the Horn of Africa and areas of the Indian Ocean as well as the Eastern Atlantic and the tip of Greenland. To cover such an area and even maintain a minimum presence and patrol required a new direction to be taken in maritime strategy. Overseas bases required a new and urgent focus. The Russian interest centred from 1969 on the Somali port of Berbera, in response to their fears that the Arabian Sea was becoming a zone of operation for Polaris vessels. Another set of problems concerned the transit times to the American seaboard. In the critical year of 1969 the Soviet Navy reappeared in the Caribbean in strength. The leasing of base facilities to provide logistic support for submarines at Cienfuegos in Cuba gave the Russians considerable advantages, for it placed the main US naval bases of Norfolk and Charleston within a two-day transit time.

From this time on a number of new Soviet warships began to appear. A longer range version of the *Yankee* class was announced in the *Delta* boats which could also be used to phase out the now ageing *Hotel* class Ballistic missile submarines. The new *Kresta* (Mark II) cruiser[19] made its appearance as a much larger and more sophisticated vessel than the Mark I version. This multi-purpose helicopter anti-submarine cruiser has a new missile in place of the Shaddock system, now there is the SSN10 with a horizon range of twenty-nine miles and a supersonic speed. In the ship-killing role these multi-purpose cruisers must represent a formidable threat to the Western navies.

Thus the Soviet navy of today is the one which has evolved as a result of the policy decisions taken more than ten years ago. These ships were developed to meet the combat needs and to counter the threat as the Soviet naval hierachy saw it at that time. There are a number of observations which can be made from these policy decisions:

First, the major surface units, such as the *Krestas* and *Kyndas* together with their attendant destroyers, are required, it would seem, to counter surprise attacks on a concentrated deployment rather than in sustained operations in a hostile environment. This marks a major shift away from the classical roles of cruisers in naval warfare and their wide range, diversity of weapon systems and design characteristics support this conclusion.

Secondly the Russians have not constructed a balanced fleet on the Western pattern and neither do any of their ships (with one exception) reflect Western designs. There is instead a heavy emphasis on submarines and these, together with many of the surface ships, are quite rigidly divided into specific tasks or missions. Also in contrast to the Western navies the Soviet fleet does have a heavy reliance on other branches of the armed forces to help support it in its missions.

By the end of the decade the Soviet Union had dramatically emerged out of the shadows of mediocrity as a naval power to rank among the leading maritime states in the visible exercise of the prerogatives of seapower. The most important task of the Soviet Navy is still that of countering the Western superiority in seaborne strategic delivery systems. In quality the Russians still lag far behind in many crucial areas of maritime technology; by the early seventies the United States had for example, equipped its nuclear submarines with a new multiple warhead missile.[20] Nevertheless the Soviet Union can now claim to being capable of deploying a naval strength more in harmony with its own new-found status as a super power.

SOVIET SUBMARINES 1972

(Office of the Chief of Naval Operations, Washington DC, April 1972)

(UNCLASSIFIED)

	Number	*Classes*
1 *Cruise Missile Subs*		
Nuclear	37	EC
Diesel	28	JW
2 *Ballistic Missile Subs*		
Nuclear	35	HY
Diesel	20	GZ
3 *Attack Submarines*		
Nuclear	28	MV
Diesel	197	FGWRRB

Notes

1. In 1963 the number of aircraft carriers on the active list of the US Navy was thirty.

2. The US Airforce operated out of Wheeler Air Force Base in Libya and in the Pacific (and excluding those bases in Indo China) the principal fields were in Guam and the Philippines.

3. The *USS Enterprise* displaced 89,600 tons full load and carried a complement of over 90 aircraft. The *USS Forrestal* was slightly smaller displacing 78,000 tons and carrying 80 aircraft. There are three other ships in this class: *Saratoga, Ranger* and *Independence.*

4. The Talos air defence missile has been used off Vietnam where it has successfully intercepted hostile aircraft at a range of 110 Km. It can have a high explosive or nuclear warhead and flies at a speed of Mach 2.5.

5. The port of Valona in Albania; see Chapter VII, pp. 83–4, for a more detailed account.

6. The *Enterprise* with the nuclear-powered frigate *Bainbridge* and the cruiser *Long Beach* provided an all-nuclear task-force.

7. See Appendix 2 for more detailed description of these air-to-surface weapon systems.

8. This involved the resignation of the Navy Minister, Christopher Mayhew.

9. One of the youngest officers ever to reach flag-rank in the Soviet Navy (at the age of thirty-two, he was appointed to the Command of the Navy in 1957.)

10. The Shaddock missile SS-N-3, the NATO code name, is more usually applied to the Army version. It has a Kiloton nuclear warhead and a range between 22/830 Km (450 nm).

11. It was a *Kashin* class destroyer, suitably stripped of all its 'sensitive' equipment, which recently visited Britain.

12. *Ethan Allen* class SSBNs built between 1959/63, displacing 7,900 tons; there are five ships of this class.

13. The *Serb* missile, the SS-N-5, requires a surface launch. The Russians claimed a range of 700 nm.

14. An excellent weapon system, SS-N-7, of which the American *Harpoon* missile will be the Western equivalent.

15. The Russians rate them as large anti-submarine cruisers. See Appendix I for more detailed account, description and classification.

16. *Oberon* and *Porpoise* class of the Royal Navy. There are thirteen vessels in commission and a number have been sold to other navies: Australia (4), Brazil (2), Chile (2) and Canada (3).

17. *Alligator* class LST (eight in service) displacing 5,800 tons full load while the *Polnocny* class LCT of 1,000 tons are typical vessels. The latter are also to be found in the Polish (20) and Indian Navies (4); the Russians have 50 in commission.

18. Especially with the Baltic Fleet where they also serve in a training capacity.

19. *Kresta II* now classed as a CG (See Appendix 3) displaces 7,500 tons; there are currently two in service.

20. Poseidon C3 missile is a MIRV—Multiple Independently-targetted Re-entry Vehicle—has a 10 x 50 KT warhead.

CHAPTER SIX

Mission Strategy and Soviet Foreign Policy in the 1970s

'The Soviet Armed Forces, including the navy, are one of the instruments of Soviet foreign policy. The inspirers of the arms race have found themselves faced with even more complex problems as a result of the establishment of our navy in the oceans of the world. But there is another side to the question: with the appearance of the Soviet navy in the oceans of the world, our ships are more and more to be seen in foreign ports, carrying out the role of political representatives of the country of socialism. In the last three years alone about a thousand Soviet ships have visited the ports of sixty countries, and more than 200,000 sailors and officers have visited the shores of foreign states.'

These brave words spoken in 1972, by Commander-in-Chief of the Soviet Navy, Admiral Gorshkov, illustrate beyond doubt that the Russian fleet is destined to play a new and positive role in foreign policy. Gorshkov, who has held flag rank for more than thirty years, has been publishing articles over the last decade, spelling out the role he envisages for the Soviet Navy.[1] As I have tried to show in the preceding chapter the Soviet Navy has not evolved according to the Western example but has instead been developed along rather unique lines in order to meet the requirements of their mission strategy as perceived by Moscow. Mission strategy, I believe, can be divided into three main areas of operation for the Soviet Union, although much of this analysis, in the absence of documentary evidence, must be conjecture. Even the stirring words of Admiral Gorshkov cannot be taken at face value since they must contain some elements of propaganda, and the reactions of various schools of thought within the more learned naval circles of the Kremlin have also to be taken into account.

The Soviet Navy shares with the United States Navy the mission of strategic deterrence as a primary task. This means the construction and deployment of the right type of ballistic missile-armed nuclear-powered submarines (SSBNs). In the Soviet case the *Yankee* class are still being constructed—there are at present about thirty-three in commission—and they are complemented by the new *Delta* class with a missile range of more than 4,000 nautical miles.[2] The Soviet Union, it is believed, is building SSBNs at the rate of seven a year which will mean that by 1977 the Deltas and Delta II will be in commission and the older *Hotels* and *Golfs* will then be phased out of service. In accordance with the Strategic Arms Limitation Talks (SALT) an agreement signed with the United States in May 1972 allows the Soviet Union to maintain 62 SSBNs and a total of 950 missiles in the fleet (33 *Yankees*, 18 *Delta* and 12 *Delta II's*). As a contributory force to the strategic nuclear balance the Polaris type of vessel has enjoyed a number of advantages for some years. Submarine-launched missiles do not as yet possess the accuracy for the delivery of a counterforce attack against the hardened missile sites of an opponent, but they are certainly accurate enough to hit sites in a counter-value strike. Submarines of this type do present problems in operational control, for example receiving instructions on targetting, or obtaining an accurate fix for navigation; yet the use of VLF (very low frequency) signals by one-way morse and inertia navigational aids is sufficient to execute a simple second strike.

The US Navy's contribution to the American strategic striking forces consists of forty-one nuclear submarines (SSBN) armed with Polaris and Poseidon ballistic missiles. Furthermore, construction has been authorised for the first of the Trident ballistic missile submarines and the first vessel of this class should become operational in 1978.[3] In the meanwhile the Poseidon armed vessels are coming into service and by the late seventies the plan is for there to be ten of these submarines. The Poseidon missile is far superior to anything the Soviet Union has yet been able to deploy and they are mounted in the *La Fayette* class Fleet Ballistic Missile submarine (FBMs). These submarines have a submerged displacement of 8,250 tons and, with a complement of 147 men, have a speed underwater in excess of thirty knots; each ship carries sixteen missiles. The Poseidon missile has a launch weight of thirty-two tons which is equivalent to a Minuteman ICBM, and has a large warhead capsule with various combinations of MIRVs and decoys. Targets for such a force are plentiful for there are 200 Soviet cities which have a population of over 100,000 and the total urban population of the Soviet Union is 50 million people. It is a brutal truth that the Poseidon is reckoned by the American analysts to be eight times more potent than the Polaris A3 missile. By the 1980's the Soviet Union in its *Delta* class vessels will have some degree of parity with the United States, especially when one takes into account the fact that the Atlantic seaboard is increasingly becoming one enormous vulnerable, urban sprawl.

Thus it is not difficult to see why both countries place so much faith in this form of nuclear delivery. An SLBM launched within 200 miles of the shore would have a flight path which is so short that no effective ABM could intercept; the threat posed by both sides is very real. By the same token such submarines are still relatively secure from even the most advanced and sophisticated anti-submarine warfare techniques. For example for ASW to offer any real threat it would have to reach a technical standard of efficiency far more lethal than any reached during the Second World War. In May 1943, the period of noted victory for Allied ASW, U-Boat losses were still less than one per cent and U-Boats *sought encounter* rather than attempted to avoid contact. Under most circumstances nuclear boats are infinitely superior to their wartime antecedents for they are capable of diving to depths of 2,000 feet whereas the maximum depth in 1943 was just under 800 feet. In terms of endurance the U-Boat could, under the most favourable circumstances, remain submerged for a maximum period of forty-eight hours whereas the modern nuclear vessel has unlimited endurance. Hard evidence is, of course, difficult to come by but it is generally believed that Western anti-submarine techniques are far superior to those of the Soviet Union. The problems are more complex than most laymen appreciate: the main emphasis is still acoustic and even so there would have to be a significant technological breakthrough by one side before the other would feel that its submarine missile force had become compromised and thus vulnerable.

To return to Soviet mission strategy: the task of the rest of the Red Navy is to ensure the credibility and operational viability of the ballistic missile submarines. In tactical terms this comes down to guaranteeing access for the Soviet SSBNs to the patrol areas from which missiles could then be launched on the United States. This role can also be interpreted as one of disrupting Western ASW in key areas especially these narrow stretches of water which are called choke points. In this sense almost every class of surface vessel are described as anti-submarine ships. Thus the *Kynda* class cruisers are designated *Bolshoy Protivo Lodochny Korabl*—Large Anti-submarine Ship—and a similar nomenclature is given to the *Moskva*. At first this was seen as a device (by the West) to circumvent the requirements of the Montreux Convention[4] which governs the movement of foreign warships through Turkish territorial waters of the Dardanelles, but this is not the case.

The second mission for the Soviet Navy has been described by Western analysts as that of 'Sea Denial'. Here, I believe, lies the clue to the reason why the Soviet Union has not developed a navy on the traditional pattern that we associate with a major power. The Russians are not interested in command of the sea along the lines of the thesis expounded by Mahan and other Western naval thinkers. Russia is a country which is not dependent on maritime lines of communication, and has little need to import goods on any significant scale by sea. The Soviet Union can reach all of its major allies without recourse to the sea and therefore they aim to deny the sea to others in particular parts of the world. This means a number of things, of which a strong, close-in defence of the four fleet areas plays an essential role. In this category long-range shore-based aviation plays a major part. The Soviet Air arm (*Morskaya Aviatsiya*) has been extensively rearmed and re-equipped with the *Tupolev 16 Badger* armed with a stand-off anti-ship missile[5] and supported by the *Bear* long-range reconnaissance aircraft providing the over-horizon link. At the same time the nuclear-powered hunter-killer submarines (SSNs) are primarily seen as operating in support of this particular mission.

The re-orientation of the Red Navy to the mission strategy which has been outlined has called for a major programme of rationalisation of the submarine strength. Sea denial, in terms of denying Western nuclear fleets sea-lines of communication which might have had an important impact on the outcome of a war on the European or Asian continent, has declined in importance, and the older diesel classes of submarines have for the most part been withdrawn from service and not replaced. Thus the overall result of the Soviet submarine programme is that the number in commission has been considerably reduced when compared to the force of the fifties, but it is now a more modern fleet. Mission strategy of Red Navy submarines in 1972 can be broken down as follows:

30 per cent of the 345 submarines on active service are nuclear-powered.
20 per cent are cruise missile in the anti-shipping role.
15 per cent ballistic missile launching types.
65 per cent attack submarines, anti-shipping and ASW.

Finally the Soviet Navy is increasingly asserting its presence in strategically important ocean areas. Before 1967 there was no significant 'Blue Water' presence but thereafter there was a move out into the North-East Atlantic and North-West Pacific in connection with large-scale Fleet exercises, and this was then followed by an extensive presence in the Mediterranean. In the years between 1968–70 Russian warships were observed in the Indian Ocean, the Caribbean, and the West African Coast, but since that date the presence in terms of submarines has declined in favour of surface combatants, auxiliaries and amphibious warfare ships.

Our inventory of Soviet warships is almost complete. However, before I turn to a closer examination of Soviet naval activity in the four fleet areas there are just three remaining surface warships which merit discussion. The first is the new aircraft carrier of the *Kuril* class. At the time of writing the lead ship of this class, the *Kiev*,[6] has yet to make its appearance, undoubedly dramatic, from the confines of its Black Sea work-up to its first operational cruise with the Northern Fleet. Our knowledge to date of this latest edition to the Red Navy would suggest that she displaces some 40,000 tons and will in all probability operate a combination of VTOL aircraft and anti-submarine helicopters in equal numbers from her flight deck.[7] Again the designation of the ship by the Russians (the Montreux convention apart) gives us a clue to her operational role, *Protivo Lodochny Kreyser* means anti-submarine cruiser. Western reports suggest the ship is armed with the full array of anti-submarine weapons, including variable depth sonar, a hull-mounted sonar and anti-submarine rocket-launchers, showing that the Soviets are taking the submarine threat seriously. A second ship of this class the *Minsk* is at present fitting out in yards at Nikolayev[8] but there is considerable doubt as to how many of these ships the Russians actually plan to deploy. With the emphasis increasingly on a world-wide deployment clearly two ships are insufficient when allowance is made for maintenance and periods of refit.

Ships of this design and appearance have an undoubted value in peace-time, and their contribution to the political impact of the Soviet Navy is an asset which the Russians would surely be determined to exploit. It is therefore not improbable that a minimum of four or even six will be built over the next ten years.

It is reasonable to suppose that the *Kuril* class will form the nucleus of task-forces capable of operating considerable distances from Soviet bases over a sustained period of time. In this context the new escort-type vessels, to complement the carrier, are already beginning to appear: there is the brand-new *Kara* class cruiser, known as the 'Swinging Frigate' in the Red Navy, and developed from the *Kresta* design.[9] The first, the *Nikolayev*, has already made one cruise with the Mediterranean squadron and since it displaces about 10,000 tons it is the first large cruiser to join the Soviet fleet since the conventionally gun-armed 'Sverdlovs' in the fifties. By any standard this cruiser packs a mighty punch,[10] and ship for ship out-matches any warship in the Western Navies. The array of missiles, air-defence systems, conventional guns, and anti-submarine weaponry which has been crammed into the not insignificant hull of 10,000 tons almost defies the imagination. Speculation would suggest that a price has had to be paid and thus the quality and comfort of crew habitation is open to question. Quality of life at sea is in proportion to a society on land, and one would not expect to see Western standards on a Soviet ship using conscript seamen. Nevertheless even for a Russian ship there must be a minimum standard to ensure combat efficiency. It can be safely assumed that there is little room on board for any re-load capacity for the main missile systems. Whereas this would be seen as a disadvantage in the Western World it is entirely in keeping with the Soviet philosophy of the decisive engagement at sea.

In support there is a new and impressive escort, the *Krivak* class destroyer, which is, in my opinion, the most handsome ship that the Soviet Union has designed; it displaces some 5,000 tons and is armed with an impressive combination of weapons.[11] Five ships of this class have so far become operational and there are at least another two under construction; they are powered by gas turbines and have the same type of missiles as the larger cruisers of the Soviet Fleet.

It has been seen that in the years since the end of the Second World War, the Red Navy has changed out of all recognition to the point where it is now, in the mid-seventies, capable of projecting power and influence abroad as an instrument of foreign policy. It is therefore expedient to examine in more detail the nature of the foreign policy which the Fleet is destined to serve. Western analysts of contemporary trends in Russian foreign policy draw our attention to the fact that the Soviet relationship with the outside world is still in an evolutionary stage. If foreign policy is defined as the promotion and protection of the national interest, then that of the Soviet Union is deeply involved with questions of defence and economics. Much of present Soviet diplomatic activity is opportunist in the manner in which it is conducted, and as recent events in Southern Africa have revealed is incredibly difficult to assess or predict in any positive way. In any list of priorities the Russians undoubtedly see the United States as the primary focus of attention; this is because the Kremlin's first interest is for the security of the homeland and the United States is seen as the only state which has a greater military capability than the Soviet Union.[12] Over the years these two great powers have gradually evolved a precarious relationship which has moved away from the hostile confrontation and propaganda-seeking summits of the fifties into a more subtle détente.

This process was speeded up in the Nixon period and became institutionalised in a number of areas of activity. Once the United States had acknowledged Soviet parity in the nuclear field, after 1968, safeguards designed to minimise the risk of nuclear collision were brought into play. In the first instance these took the form of the strategic arms limitation talks (SALT) which in 1972 placed a quantitative limit on nuclear delivery systems. Secondly through a series of regular and private meetings, invariably at Secretary of State level, a system of crisis management techniques was hammered out. This involved a mutual recognition of vital interests in various parts of the world where client-states were in danger of upsetting the fragile balance of power which existed between the super powers.[13] Finally the United States has sought to entangle the Soviet Union in a web of trade agreements which, together with other factors, have the effect of constraining Soviet behaviour in the interests of world peace.[14] To the American, détente means an adversary relationship, it is a relaxation, a means of normalizing relations between the two powers. But 'normalization' in this sense involves what Henry Kissinger has defined on a number of occasions as a 'relationship of moderated tension'. The relaxation has come through a re-definition and better understanding of each other's intentions, whereas military capability (within the safeguards of

SALT) remains at a very high level. Détente does not mean ideological disarmament, for the United States are no nearer to accepting the Soviet way of life and the Communist distaste for capitalism is as strong as ever. What détente does offer is an alternative to the unrestricted arms race of the earlier period which when placed in a context of mutual hostilities could only have produced, in the end result, nuclear Armageddon.

Within this basic framework the Soviet version of détente is roughly similar. The Kremlin see the whole process as a tactical compromise to ward off the risk of nuclear obliteration, which cannot be in the interest of either super power. An eminent Soviet expert, Malcolm Macintosh, has described the Soviet understanding of détente in the following way: 'we welcome détente and a special relationship with you, and we want them to cover a wide variety of international activities and to become institutionalized and irreversible. We also want you to accept our definitions of parity in military strength. But you must recognize that we believe that our policies and outlook are scientifically based and historically correct: that if we seek a change in the balance of power in our favour and a move in individual countries towards regimes favourable to us, we are justified in doing so before history and our political beliefs; and you, whose policies fly in the face of history, cannot match the soundness of our views or the forward march of our influence. If you want to play the power game within the relationship, and we believe you do, we will play it too: and you may win temporary successes. But our successes will turn out to be the irreversible ones. We shall never give up our attempts to change the political alignments of countries we regard as important. If you think that détente or our new relationship will lessen the intensity of the ideological (i.e. political) struggle between us, you are making a great mistake.'[15]

Bearing this interpretation of détente in mind I should now like to examine, in the following chapters, the Soviet naval activity in the Mediterranean, Atlantic, Indian Ocean and the Pacific.

Notes

1. See in particular his series called 'Navies in War and Peace' published, in translation, by the United States Naval Institution (translator Theodore A. Neely, Jr) and edited by Herbert Preston, Colonel USMC (Ret).

2. The *Delta* class displace 9,000 tons dived and are armed with twelve SS-N-8 missiles which have a range of 4,000 nautical miles (nm). There will eventually be nineteen of these vessels in commission.

3. The *Trident* class will displace 12,000 tons submerged and be equipped with twenty-four tubes for the Trident I missile with a range of 4,000 miles and a multiple warhead.

4. See Chapter Seven, page 79.

5. Kennel/Kipper/Kett air to surface missiles, see Appendix 2.

6. See above Chapter XI for the first operational cruise of the *Kiev*.

7. It is estimated that the full complement will be 25 Hormone A or modified Hind A helicopters and 25 Vtol Freehand aircraft.

8. Black Sea shipyards.

9. The first of this class the *Nikolayev* is at sea and there is a second under construction.

10. Missile systems:—8: SS-N-10, (anti-ship cruise missiles). 4: SA-M-4, (SAM). 4: SA-N-3, (SAM). Guns:—4×76 mm; 4×30 mm. A/S weapons:— 2 16 barrelled MBU launchers. Torpedo:—10 (2×5) 21 inch.

11. Missile systems: 4 SS-N-10. 2 SA-N-4. Guns: 4×76 mm. 4×30 mm. A/S: 12 barrelled MBU launchers. Torpedo: 8 (2×4) 21 inch.

12. See Appendix 4 for military balance at sea.

13. This aspect was especially relevant to the Middle-East War of 1973 and events inside Portugal a year later.

14. This is seen in terms of what has become known as the 'Kissinger Doctrine' and the Jackson Amendment to the Wheat agreements with the Soviet Union.

15. "The Impact of the Middle East crisis on Super Power Relations". *Adelphi Paper* 114, *IISS, The Middle East and the International System*, I, *the Impact of the 1973 War*.

Part Two

CHAPTER SEVEN

The Red Navy in the Mediterranean

The foreign policy of the Soviet Union, and thus by association the projection of power at sea as an instrument of that policy, is severely constrained by geography. Russia has little in the way of ocean frontage and very few ports of any strategic significance lead directly to the open sea.[1] Instead Russian access to the sea is dominated by others, in the Mediterranean, for example, Soviet warships have first to negotiate the narrow Turkish straits. Since 1936 movement of shipping through Turkish territorial waters has been subject to the Montreux Convention, and on a number of occasions the Kremlin has attempted to revise the Treaty. The Convention is long, complicated and, like most international agreements signed by nation states, is open to differing interpretations. There is no doubt that it has caused considerable difficulties for the Soviet Union and it is therefore pertinent for us to examine its main provisions which lay down that:

1. Merchant vessels of all countries enjoy freedom of transit and navigation through the straits in time of peace or war, provided that Turkey is not belligerent, when only neutral ships may use the waters.

2. The major limitation comes in the transit of ships-of-war and in this context there are a number of restrictions:
    (a) Non-Black Sea states are particularly constrained both in the number of ships in course of transit (no more than nine) and their aggregate tonnage may not exceed 15,000 tons.

(b) There is no tonnage limitation to warships of Black Sea states and even capital ships may use the Straits provided that only one ship at a time is in transit.

(c) Submarines from Black Sea powers must negotiate the Straits on the surface.

(d) If Turkey is at war passage of warships legally is left to the discretion of Turkey.

The Montreux Convention did transfer authority from an International Commission[2] to the Government of Turkey. It was initially intended that the Treaty should operate for twenty years, and provided that no state challenged the Convention in its final two years it was to run indefinitely.

It was not until the last stages of the Second World War in Europe that the Soviet Union began to press Turkey for a revision of the Montreux Convention. In essence the Russians demanded a share in the defence of the Straits and that the terms of the Convention should be revised to allow unrestricted passage for all ships belonging to Black Sea powers. On the question of transit the Turks did indicate a willingness to reach agreement, but on the issue of the status of the Convention there could be no compromise; Turkey argued impeccably that such a major revision could only be undertaken by the original signatories. The United States and Great Britain fully supported Turkey in the battle of nerves that gradually developed with the Soviet Union in the immediate postwar period. In the summer of 1946 the *USS Missouri*, one of the mighty battleships of the Second World War, visited Istanbul as tangible proof of American solidarity. Continued Soviet pressure on Turkey, coupled with Western suspicions that Stalin was deeply implicated in the Greek Civil War, resulted in the Truman Doctrine in March 1947 and the subsequent influx of vast amounts of American Aid. Thus Turkish neutrality, which had been an essential feature of Levantine politics, and I suspect Soviet foreign policy for twenty-five years, was suddenly reversed and the Ottoman embraced the Western Alliance.[3] This, in turn, produced a particular type of American commitment to the Eastern Mediterranean and something akin to a special relationship with the Greeks and the Turks which was to survive until the early Seventies.

Although Stalin's first and only major foray into Middle-Eastern politics had in its crude and bludgeoning manner met with disaster, the Soviet Union has nevertheless persisted in its search for a sphere of influence in the Middle-Eastern World and a measure of status in the Mediterranean. Some historians and political commentators have interpreted such policy initiatives as simply those which are complementary to the expanding tastes and appetite of a developing great power. However, this explanation is too simple and we need to examine other factors to see both why the Soviet Union seeks a foreign policy in this region, and what part a Red Navy Mediterranean presence plays in their overall scheme of things.

Unlike the United States, the Soviet Union is bound to have a more permanent and a primary interest in Middle-Eastern affairs. These interests are not economic, for although Russia is the main customer for Egyptian cotton and purchases natural gas from Iran these are merely cosmetic The prime consideration is security. The Middle East landmass, often described as the 'hub of three continents' is, together with its seas, a neighbouring territory to the Soviet Union. In this way Tzarist and Soviet interests seem to be compatible: the quest for warm ports and the perennial search for a way out of the narrow seas. Even though the diplomacy was crude Stalin's behaviour was entirely consistent with that of a classical land empire seeking to secure a glacis of friendly states, a cluster of client powers to protect its southern flank. Equally consistent, though I suspect a cause for remorse was an endorsement of the embryonic Israel, in terms of a Socialist anti-British state, whose threatened birth was a source of friction within the Western camp. Thus ever since a messy foreign policy had resulted in the American presence, the Soviet Union has been waiting for the last Western visitor to the Middle East to leave. In the early years Khrushchev in particular was able to exploit Western mistakes to secure a foothold in the Middle East. Thus the attempt by a 'blinkered' Dulles to close the gap in global containment by the ill-fated MEDO (Middle East Defence Organization) and the practically still-born Baghdad Pact[4] aroused the fury of the Egyptians and the Syrians. The main instruments by which Moscow was able to operate this policy was in ever-increasing amounts of aid and especially arms. The initial deal through the Czechs as intermediaries to an Egyptian shunned by the West in 1955, was a modest affair when compared to the huge injections of weapons that followed hard on the heels of the Arab débâcle of 1967. However, to see all Soviet arms sales to the Middle East purely in terms of the Arab–Israeli conflict would be to over-state the whole question. The deal in 1955 included submarines, a weapon system which was really outside the context of Egypt's struggle with Israel. Instead one should interpret this as part of Khrushchev's initiative into the politics of the Third World through the build-up in naval strength of carefully selected states.[5]

In the early years of Khrushchev it is very hard to disentangle Soviet motives and ambitions from the hard realities of capability, except to say that no clear pattern emerges in the Middle East and Mediterranean until the naval question begins to intrude. Hitherto the Soviet Navy had only made the occasional foray out of the Black Sea into the Mediterranean Basin. In contrast the US Sixth Fleet was firmly established in the region and in July 1958 presented the Soviet Union with an awesome demonstration of the projection of power from the sea. The Government of the Lebanon appealed to the United States for military assistance against what was perceived to be a Communist inspired rebellion.[6] Within twenty hours of the original request 1,800 marines landed ashore from a naval task-force while carrier-based aircraft ensured the integrity of the operation. Khrushchev and his advisers were confronted with dramatic evidence of the short fall and inadequacy of the Soviet Union to influence such events. As at the time of the ill-fated Anglo-French armada at Suez two years previously, Khrushchev could do little more than make diplomatic noises off-stage. The United States had demonstrated that the Eastern Mediterranean was a 'mare nostrum' in terms of the operation of the Sixth Fleet, and this in terms of threats to the Soviet Union was reinforced by a number of other factors. To the expanding nuclear capability of the Sixth Fleet Carriers was added the series of bilateral arrangements which the United States conducted with a number of friendly powers that lay within bomber range of Russia. In Turkey, Saudi Arabia, Pakistan and Libya strategic air command bombers were deployed with their nuclear payloads ready to strike deep into the heart of the Soviet Union. Only with those states in the area who deliberately stood apart from the American scheme of things, Egypt and Syria, could the Soviet Union attempt to build a relationship and thus seek a way out of the restraining grasp of containment.

In 1958 the Soviet Union was able to negotiate base facilities with their uneasy Communist satellite Albania. Within a short time the Red Navy, in this its first sanctuary outside the confines of Soviet territory, quickly established a modest presence. Up to eight *Whisky* class submarines were deployed in the port of Valona together with an attendant depot ship. There was a significant increase in Soviet traffic through the Turkish straits but much of this was in the form of auxiliaries ferrying supplies to the Albanian-based submarines. At the same time modest posses of destroyers entered the Mediterranean, occasionally accompanied by a gun-cruiser, obviously with the purpose of exercising with the Valona flotilla. It is not difficult to envisage what the combat mission of these submarines would have been had hostilities between the super powers occurred: to prevent any Western reinforcement of the Turkish straits by interdicting the sea routes and to cause what damage they could to the Sixth Fleet. However, it is clear that the Russian Navy, through exercises, was building up both an operational doctrine and expertise to counter the threat of the Sixth Fleet in readiness for the day it could deploy a more battleworthy force.

The first year of crisis for the Russians in the Mediterranean was 1961. Albania, angry over many things and siding with China in the developing friction between the two main Communist powers, withdrew from the Warsaw Pact and expelled the Red Navy from its base at Valona. The loss of this secure anchorage and base facilities was important, and the Soviet Government embarked upon a feverish diplomatic initiative to find alternatives. In the Autumn of 1961 Admiral Gorshkov visited Egypt while Tito's Yugoslavia was wooed and cajoled; neither initiative produced any positive result. Russia became seriously alarmed when in 1962 the United States announced that Polaris submarines were on patrol in the Eastern Mediterranean. The immediate Soviet response was to propose that these waters should become a 'Nuclear Free Zone', and for the next year their naval activity was practically non-existent. It was not until 1964 that the Soviet Navy began to grapple seriously with the task of countering the American threat in the Mediterranean. By this time the Navy was beginning to receive the new vessels already discussed, and with a more balanced force the fleet could begin to move out for its forward deployment. In 1964 Khrushchev visited Cairo amidst a welter of publicity to try once more to secure a base for naval operations beyond the Black Sea.

The Egyptians would probably have given way in the end but they did not in 1964 and this failure undoubtedly contributed to the demise of Khrushchev. Therefore to counter the threat of the American Navy, the Russians had to resort to a forward defence in the Eastern Mediterranean, by a force which was composed of good modern ships, but which suffered from the crippling restraint of open anchorages and no base facilities. Even so the Soviet Union was able to gain some political 'spin-off', in that the appearance of a cruiser and destroyer escort coincided with the Cyprus Crisis of 1964. Turkey was warned off interfering by the United States, an event which marks the watershed in Turkish–American relations and from which they have never really recovered. The Turkish foreign minister visited Moscow soon after this incident and negotiated a substantial and favourable trade agreement. Between the years 1964–67 the Soviet Union considerably augmented its naval strength in the Eastern Mediterranean. It is reasonable to assume that the Turks, in return for the trade and aid, relaxed the restrictions imposed by the Montreux Convention. The absence of a port would have required a large number of supply ships and warships[7] operating in the Mediterranean for relatively short periods having to return home for those modest repairs which could not be undertaken in an open anchorage. The sailings through the Turkish Straits must have been excessive and had the Convention been rigidly enforced, it would have caused major problems for the Soviet Union.

From the open anchorages off Crete to the home naval bases at Odessa in the Crimea is a voyage of almost 1,500 miles, and when one takes this into consideration, with the problems outlined above, it is clear that the Soviet Navy had to surmount formidable odds and pay a heavy price to achieve its mission objectives at this time. Once on station the Soviet warships, manned by young and novice crews with a fledgling doctrine and little experience, had to operate in a hostile air environment against a force which was its better in terms of both quantity and quality. If one includes NATO air strength in the calculation, the odds which the Soviet Mediterranean squadron faced were overwhelming. That it would have been utterly destroyed is not in question; what is problematical is whether the individual ships could have survived long enough to deliver their hardware on Western ships.[8] There were a number of factors which were in favour of the Soviet Union at the time, and which to a large degree still hold true. If Russian ships had to be in range to deliver their weapons then they could shadow Western ships very closely and indeed under some circumstances the switch from a peace to wartime footing would be almost instantaneous. Although the umbrella of peace did provide some cover, the morale of those Soviet officers and key crewmen who were aware of the real situation must have been low.

Nevertheless, in the years up to 1967 and the outbreak of the June War the Soviet Navy spent its time profitably in exercises, where new techniques of ASW and anti-carrier could be practised and new ships gain in competence and professional expertise. Improved performance was itself reflected in longer cruises and increased numbers of ships on station.

The June War of 1967 which allowed the Soviet Navy to resolve one set of problems led to a completely different type of restraint. The super powers were to a great extent encapsulated from the effects of the June War[9] but Russian destroyers shadowed US carriers and there was a considerable increase in the number of Soviet Warships on station in the Mediterranean through that month. Initially the massive defeat of Arab arms could not have done much for the Soviet reputation in Cairo and Damascus since the Arabs had used Russian equipment and, presumably, tactics. However, any feelings of resentment that the Arab leaders might feel had to be tempered with the more pressing need to re-arm, and Russia was the only source for an arms transfusion on the scale required by the humiliated Arabs. The Russian terms quickly became self-evident when in July Soviet warships steamed into Port Said and Alexandria, ostensibly to provide cover against further Israeli airattack.

In terms of naval deployments in the Mediterranean the years from 1967 to the Soviet expulsion from Egypt in 1972 produced a new situation. Base facilities allowed, for the first time, year-round deployments and more ships could be maintained on station. At the same time the awesome might of the Western air threat had, at least in Soviet eyes, been reduced by the appearance of the squadron of missile-armed warships, and the deployment from Egyptian air bases of long-range bombers, some of which were equipped with anti-ship missiles.

Thus if one looks at the Soviet pattern of deployment during these years the following picture would emerge. Intelligence gatherers (AGIs), usually specially equipped trawlers, were operating off the coast of America, a Polaris submarine was based at Rota in Spain, while others were observing traffic in the Sicilian channel and keeping a close watch on the main American fleet anchorage in the Bay of Naples. There would probably be a third deployment off the Israeli coast monitoring Israeli communications. Under average conditions and normal activity, one would find Soviet warships following virtually established patrol patterns in both the Sicilian channel and in the entrance to the Aegean Sea. However, when American task-forces put to sea, and especially when such a force included a carrier, then Soviet warships would be found in close attendance. Throughout this phase of deployment, Soviet shadowing of American vessels often took an aggressive form causing the former often to make emergency changes of course to avoid collision. Such harassment was also accompanied by diplomatic offensives on the part of the Kremlin, claiming the American presence in the Eastern Mediterranean to be a deliberate provocation to the Soviet Union. Such escapades had the rather forlorn aim of persuading Washington to pull out of the Mediterranean, or at least reduce the sorties into the Eastern Basin. When not on patrol the Soviet warships would be in one of the Egyptian ports or moored to a permanent buoy in one of the fleet anchorages. These anchorages, for reasons of security and also reflecting the need to be able to respond quickly to a hot war situation, were strategically dispersed throughout the Mediterranean. Thus a small anchorage was maintained east of the Straits of Gibraltar (Millila Point, Alboran Island). To cover the Sicilian channel Soviet warships were moored in the Gulf of Hammamet and the Hurd Bank. The main fleet anchorages were off the island of Crete and to the East of Cyprus.

Once the *Moskva* had made her dramatic and well orchestrated appearance in 1968 accompanied as she was by the cries of an alarmist Western press, Soviet naval exercises took on a new shape and dimension in the Mediterranean. Invariably their theme was anti-submarine as the fleet practised in conjunction with helicopters and the heavier aircraft from the Egyptian air bases. All but major refitting and repair work was undertaken at the Egyptian ports, of which the most important was the Qabbari shipyard in Alexandria. There were in addition storage depots at both Alexandria and Port Said, while further to the West the port of Mersa Matruh was developed as a deep-water harbour.

It is very difficult to say how many warships the Russians maintain in the Mediterranean simply because maximum figures can be explained in terms of overlap between relieving and homeward-bound vessels. Throughout a year there would be somewhere between 10–14 surface warships and possibly 8 or 12 submarines. This figure would obviously increase in the event of a major crisis when, for example, in 1970 during the Jordanian crisis (Black September) there were 23 surface and 15 submarines on station. By the same token large-scale NATO exercises would attract a fair measure of Soviet activity.

In the vast majority of cases Soviet deployments in the Mediterranean were sustained by the Black Sea Fleet, although it was not unusual for the Baltic and Northern Fleets to send warships on passage to the Mediterranean and vice-versa. Operations of this type enabled the Red Fleet to attempt to remedy its glaring deficiency in the technique of replenishment at sea.

The wartime role of the Mediterranean squadron remained the same throughout the sixties, namely to prevent the West closing in on the Turkish Straits and to counter the threat of the Sixth Fleet. It is reasonable to assume that their skills and capabilities in these roles improved with time and with the arrival of new and better ships in greater numbers. In addition the units had a political role while cruising in peacetime: 'Showing the Flag' exercises have the additional advantage of creating an impression that the American monopoly is broken and thus the rising tide of naval power belongs to the Soviet Union. Objectives such as these, aimed in a precise manner for local consumption are helped by the fact that before 1973 there were very few Arab ports in the Mediterranean that would entertain an American warship.

In terms of a peacetime situation the Western press have on a number of occasions drawn attention to the Soviet role as being that of inhibiting or constraining any American projection of naval power ashore, along the lines of the Lebanon in 1958.[10] Their case is reinforced by the low-key American activity in the recent Lebanese crisis,[11] but this is assuming that the United States sought intervention and then was deterred by the Soviet presence. Any such assumption does not take into account the domestic political situation in the United States, changing strategic priorities, and the immobility of the State Department in the final stages of the Presidential election process. For these reasons alone any such assumption about the Sixth Fleet and its capabilities is made invalid. By the same token many would claim that the Soviet navy constrained American activity in those Arab states, such as Syria and Egypt, which were major recipients of Soviet aid. To propose this thesis is to ignore the fact that prior to the October War of 1973 there were clearly demarcated spheres of influence which were rigidly adhered to by the Super Powers in terms of their respective client states. Thus this form of naval activity could only have worked in the very few peripheral states in the region that did not belong to either camp, such as Algeria[12] and Tunisia.

Therefore by the October War one cannot escape the conclusion that the purveyor of Soviet influence in the Mediterranean was not the Red Fleet but the arms agreements. It is in this area that the Soviet Union increasingly came to pay a new and heavier price for its naval presence. If the cost in the earlier sixties was seen in logistic and operational terms, then by the seventies the Russians found themselves drawn deeper and deeper into the entanglements of Arab politics. The Kremlin held on grimly and weathered the storms of fraternal squabbles, while all the time dependent upon the few advantages accruing from the sale of arms to the Middle East.[13] This is a form of diplomacy which is highly suspect in its projection, and something which Western powers had long since learned was of dubious value as a means of promoting a sphere of influence.

In July 1972, the inevitable happened when the Soviet Union fell from grace in Egypt, and their armed forces and installations were expelled and closed down. The complicated events which gave rise to this decision lie beyond the confines of this book, except to say that Sadat had found in his rapprochement with Saudi Arabia a ready source of wealth that carried certain anti-Soviet strings, which when combined with the unwillingness of the Russians to accept a presence under the conditions set in Cairo, provided sufficient reason for this action. At a stroke the Soviet navy lost the facilities at Alexandria and elsewhere, and were thus forced back onto their own resources. It took the navy almost three years to dismantle the apparatus of their presence, in particular the heavy repair facilities, but it caused immense strains on their fledgling float support resources. A depot ship of the *Don* class[14] moved into the permanent anchorage off Crete to act as the headquarters ship and communications centre for the Mediterranean presence, but the repair line stretched once again into the Black Sea.

Soviet influence in the Middle East has been on the wane since the death of Nasser, despite the growing visible strength of the naval presence. The October War hastened the process when the navy had to conform to the demands of Russian détente with the United States. There was an increase in naval activity and Soviet ships had been used prior to the war to lift North African contingents into Syria. The bulk of re-supply for the shattered Egyptian and Syrian armies was undertaken by the heavy lift capability of the Soviet Air Force. When the war produced a super power confrontation on 26th/27th October, the Soviet threat to send combat units into Egypt was immediately countered by an

American strategic alert. Confronted by a determination of this magnitude the Soviet leadership almost immediately backed down and ran for cover. The Red Navy, despite all the boasting of Gorshkov, was but an insignificant pawn in the super power game and quite incapable of influencing events which were seen to be contrary to the interests of the United States. Although nothing more than a witness to the military acts of the October War, the Red Navy then suffered a more direct humiliation and assault on its prestige in the events which came about in the succeeding months. Following on the Kissinger initiatives and disengagement, the operation to clear the Suez Canal and re-open this once vital waterway to international shipping became a viable proposition. In keeping with the Soviet image of the Mediterranean as a 'mare nostrum' this should have been exclusively their task. However, the Americans carried out the preliminary salvage operation and were responsible for repairing the banks of the canal, while the Royal Navy cleared the explosives from the Canal itself. The Soviet Navy's role was limited to removing the minefield which they themselves had laid in the Red Sea entrance and the Gulf of Suez. Perhaps the unkindest cut of all for the Russians was to see 'Old Glory' and the White Ensign flying over a theatre of operations for which they had always entertained an exclusive ambition.

It is ironic that now, when the Soviet Navy has at last managed to overcome all the hurdles set in its path and achieved a naval presence in the Mediterranean which begins to measure up to its requirements, the United States Navy has reduced its commitment. In terms of the nuclear strike threat on the Soviet Union the carriers of the Sixth Fleet are less important, the nuclear bombers have long since been withdrawn from the Middle Eastern states in favour of the home-based Intercontinental Ballistic Missiles (ICBMs). Finally, the introduction of the longer range Poseidon missiles has removed the need for ballistic missile submarine patrols in these confined waters. There is still an American nuclear capability deployed in the Eastern Mediterranean, but compared with the total strategic nuclear forces it is but a small commitment and when measured against the Soviet naval effort it must raise questions of cost effectiveness for the strategists in the Kremlin. The Sixth Fleet has lost much of its credibility and effectiveness in the Mediterranean over the last few years, but this has not been caused by the growing strength of the Russian Navy. Rather one looks for an answer to such trends as the leftward swing in the domestic politics of Portugal,

Italy and Greece together with the events in Cyprus. There are still major problems that are as yet unresolved and which do form part of the incomplete agenda of Middle Eastern and Mediterranean affairs. The future of a strategically important country such as Yugoslavia after Tito and the problems which will confront the Mediterranean members of NATO in terms of alignment does give cause for concern. It is not difficult to envisage this area as a major source of instability in the near future and it would be quite wrong to deny any role or influence that the Soviet Navy could exert over events. But even for the Russian Navy these are of a secondary nature except in an extreme situation and one would anticipate the fleet using the Mediterranean essentially as a means of access to the oceans of the world. Those events and needs which first brought the Red Fleet into the Mediterranean have declined in importance as the focus of confrontation with the maritime nuclear forces of the United States centres on the open waters of the oceans of the world.

Notes

1. The only port of any significance is Petro-Pavlovsk in the Kamchatka Peninsula at the Soviet Pacific Provinces.

2. The International Commission for the Straits dates back to 24 July 1923 when as a result of the first conference convened at Lausanne to settle the question of passage through the Bosphorous and Dardanelles. The commission, under the chairmanship of Turkey, demilitarised the Straits and gave freedom of passage to warships 'under any banner'. These arrangements suited neither Turkey nor Russia, hence the Montreux Convention.

3. Turkey, whose forces participated in the Korean War under the United Nations banner, joined the North Atlantic Alliance at the same time as Greece, in September 1951. Turkey formally acceded to the Treaty on 18 February 1952.

4. The Baghdad Pact began life as the Turko-Iraqi Pact signed on 24 February 1955. It was the first link in the American-sponsored 'Northern tier of containment' in the Middle East. Later Great Britain joined followed by Pakistan and Iran. The overthrow of the Hashemite Monarchy of Iraq in 1958 led to Iraq formally withdrawing on 24 March 1958. Meanwhile the headquarters had been transferred to Ankara and the name of the Alliance changed to the Central Treaty Organization (CENTO).

5. Another recipient of Soviet aid was Indonesia which by 1966 had received in naval forces:

> 1 *Sverdlov* class cruiser (renamed *Irian*)
> 7 *Skoryi* class destroyers
> 7 *Riga* class frigates
> 8 Patrol boats of the *Kronstadt* class and a host of small craft.

At the same time 'Janes' list Soviet-supplied warships to the Egyptian Navy as:

> 8 *Whisky* class submarines
> 6 *Skoryi* destroyers and a number of minesweepers/patrol craft/missile boats.

6. Nasser and Egypt were believed (by the West) to have sponsored the attemped coup.

7 A typical squadron in 1966 would have comprised:

> 2/4 diesel submarines
> 3/5 destroyers/escorts
> a *Sverdlov* cruiser/Depot ship.

8. The Soviet Union saw their missile-equipped warships as being capable of surviving for what Gorshkov frequently refers to as the 'Battle of the first Salvo'.

9. Although the *USS Liberty*, technically listed as a Research Ship, (AGTE) was severely damaged by Israeli air and torpedo-boat attack in the Eastern Mediterranean on 8 June 1967.

10. Civil War broke out between the rival factions of Christian and Muslims in the Lebanon 1958. The Christian President appealed to the United States for help in restoring law and order. U.S. Marines from the Mediterranean Fleet stormed ashore at Beirut and restored the situation.

11. June/July 1976.

12. The Algerian Navy of light forces and patrol craft has Osa and *Komar* class missile boats.

13. For an inventory of Soviet military equipment in both the Egyptian and Syrian armed forces by October 1973, see Military Balance (IISS). The list below gives just some indication of the scale and extent:

> Egypt had some 1,800 battle tanks and an airforce of over 600 combat planes.
> Syria had more than 2,000 Soviet battle tanks and an airforce of 400 combat planes.

14. Six *Don* class depot ships, each one displacing some 9,000 tons full load, were all constructed between 1957–62.

CHAPTER EIGHT

Northern Deployments

Except for the occasional sortie from the Mediterranean, or the odd ship en route from the Pacific the Soviet warships, which patrol off Western shores or are observed in the Atlantic, are stationed in either the Baltic or the Barents Sea. Of the two naval commands, the bigger and more important is the Northern Fleet which operates out of the Kola Inlet and comes under the jurisdiction of the Murmansk military district.

Until recent years the northern flank of NATO was considered to be 'Europe's quiet corner'. It was not unaffected by the tensions of super-power confrontation to the South, but the territorial status quo was maintained by a delicate balance of political and military considerations. Now this once tranquil state of affairs is slowly changing. The North is in metamorphosis. There seem to be two essential considerations which are exerting a new and destabilising influence: in the first instance there is the discovery, and one assumes eventual exploitation, of potentially huge resources of natural gas and oil along Norway's continental shelf. The second, and on which I wish to concentrate, is the remarkable qualitative and quantitative growth of Soviet military power in adjacent waters and contiguous land areas.

For some time the Kola Inlet has contained the single largest concentration of Soviet maritime strength. This Northern Fleet is believed to consist of fifty-six major surface warships, 160 submarines, of which approximately half are nuclear powered; it is estimated that close to seventy per cent of the Soviet SSBNs are based in the Kola Inlet. There is in addition a regiment of naval infantry together with the attendant landing craft and support vessels. 'Such a concentration of force is made possible because the warm waters of the Gulf Stream keep the fjords and ports in Northern Europe ice-free as far east as Murmansk. The necessity for such a deployment is conditioned by the strategic value of these northern waters in this age of confrontation between the super powers. The Arctic tip of Europe lies directly on the shortest route between the most densely populated centres of the United States and the Soviet Union. At the present time this has a strategic value and significance in terms of surveillance, early warning systems, and defence mechanisms, against inter-continental ballistic missile attack. As the sea-based deterrent increasingly becomes the core of the super power central balance, the Kola peninsular will emerge as the basket where an ever increasing number of Soviet strategic eggs are located.

Western analysis sees the prime function of the Northern fleet as contributory to the strategic missions of the ballistic missile submarines. At one time this was interpreted as moving to a forward deployment in the critical seas around the Iceland–UK 'gap' and the Denmark Straits. These waters, controllable from a Western point of view, had to be negotiated before the Russian submarines could break through into the open seas and on to their patrol stations. At the same time these narrow channels represented the optimum point for the launch of the Western maritime strike threat on the Soviet Union. However, the more recent developments by both sides of longer range missile systems has removed these historically significant waters[1] from the focal point of the strategic balance. Today we can interpret the role of the Northern Fleet as exerting a measure of control over the Barents Sea and North Cape in order to sweep the passage clear for the SSBNs to move to their patrol stations. It is clearly the Soviet Union's intention to dominate the Barents sea, and to deny its use, militarily, to Western naval forces.

So long as the Northern Fleet can meet the priorities of its strategic mission then there is little reason to anticipate any change in the balance of power or territorial revision in this region. Clearly the Norwegians offer no threat to the Soviet Union, neither do they seek any modification in their own position or status. The Norwegian forces in the Finnmark County, and their restraints on the stationing of allied forces on their soil, are reflections of their domestic political situation and not the military threat.[2] However, the presence of amphibious forces, the stationing of naval infantry, and the use of ordinary merchant vessels as auxiliary assault ships in recent exercises, point to the Soviet option to bring about some changes in the territorial status quo in the North Cape. This, in turn, has been reflected in the number and scale of NATO exercises in Norway which have been premised on precisely this form of scenario of which 'Exercise Strong Express' was fairly typical.

It is not difficult to produce a number of situations which could prompt the Soviet Union into a *fait accompli*, a smash and grab of ports in Northern Norway. At the top of the list would be those scenarios in which the Soviet leaders saw a challenge to the security of their country, or even the integrity of their fleet operations.[3] Thus a major and spectacular breakthrough by Western technology techniques of anti-submarine warfare might easily be countered by the need to increase the base and fleet areas of operations. Secondly, in a situation where there was an increase in tension and hostility between the super powers, the Soviet Union might well feel impelled to secure and maintain the operational integrity of the largest military base in the world at Murmansk.

Yet another potential cause for friction could be at a local level and involve a direct clash with Norway over the Barents Sea. Norwegian strategists[4] point to this stretch of water in politico-military terms as one of the most important sea areas in the world simply because it is the main highway for the largest concentration of Soviet warships from the world's biggest base to the open waters of the Atlantic Ocean. Ever since the entry of Norway into NATO it has been a vital aspect of Norwegian foreign policy to keep the Soviet Union from feeling that its national interest in the Barents Sea is being threatened to the point where it might feel it necessary to take security measures against Norway. An example of this is the Svalbard Treaty[5] where the Norwegians and Russians recognise the demilitarization of the Spitzbergen (Svalbard) island chain. Hence no allied forces are ever located or allowed to deploy, even for exercise purposes, east of the line 24° of latitude.[6] However, the prospects for the immediate future contain the ingredients for a drastic change. The Continental Shelf, especially in the region of Bjørnøya and the Finnmark coast, is showing all the potential for a bonanza in natural gas and oil. Within a short time the area could become the focus of quite intense oil speculation and prospecting outfits, many of whom will be internationally crewed and multi-nationally owned. Once reserves are located they will be tapped by oil rigs and other forms of semi-permanent installations.

The Soviets are bound to fear the intrusion into these congested yet vital waters of intelligence devices which can monitor naval activity[7]. Much will depend upon the state of affairs elsewhere but the degree of Soviet sensitivity over this issue could produce an aggressive response.

These are just some of a number of scenarios which could confront the Atlantic Alliance with a hot war situation on its Northern flank. They all reflect Soviet sensitivity over the role and operational integrity of the Northern Fleet. At the same time other opinions in the Western world would emphasise that this fleet itself is a destabilizing factor. Such is its priority in Soviet defence that its interests are bound to be reflected in the highest and most influential echelons of the High Command. It is not difficult, nor is it implausible, to imagine a situation in which the super powers were in the throes of a crisis and conflict seemed likely; the naval lobby could put telling pressure on the leadership to pre-empt in the North, to protect the integrity of Northern Fleet operations. Professor John Erickson succinctly talks in terms of the 'Russians striking first in the last resort.[8]

So any Soviet *fait accompli* in the Northern region is not seen simply in terms of territorial aggrandisement, but rather as a reflection of the needs and security of its maritime interests. This implies in any of the scenarios outlined above a modest and limited objective, but when interpreted into territory it places a completely different complexion on affairs. Any military operation, be it a reflection of the need to guarantee the offensive operation in the Atlantic or the protection of the Kola bases, must, to be meaningful, require the acquisition of all Norwegian territory at least as far west as Tromsö. Such an advance would need to embrace the strategically vital airfield at Bardufoss which is over 600 miles from the Soviet frontier. In the normal peacetime situation the Soviet army deploys just two motorised divisions in this area, and although both are of category A in terms of readiness they are obviously inadequate, even with the naval infantry as reinforcement. They clearly would need reinforcements of at least one division before any operation could be undertaken and it is this warning on which NATO is relying to move the necessary reinforcements of their own into the area.[9] Even a three divisional assault plus the support of the Northern Fleet would still present the Russians with considerable problems. All operations would have to be in range of Soviet airfields and they would even then not have the close-in support capability on the lines of US Marine combat squadrons, which the West regard as an indispensable element of amphibious assault. Finally, NATO commentators point to another major Soviet weakness in the absence of the necessary logistical and combat engineer support for landing operations. So although a Soviet capability for amphibious warfare is present with the Northern Fleet it is seen to have major limitations and can only be intended in the most limited sense for it is short-legged in its capability.

Despite these limitations, if the ingredients are present, a Soviet 'smash and grab raid' on Northern Norway is a distinct possibility. If it happens it will quickly become a race between the Soviet advance and Norwegian and Western response. If the two Soviet divisions are reinforced by an airborne division then that crucial political warning time, around which much Western planning must hinge, will be critically reduced. It is not implausible to say that under certain conditions Finnmark could be overwhelmed before NATO has time to react. NATO consultation can be a long drawn-out process and if there was a tardy deployment of Ace Mobile Force then the Russians might possibly achieve their objectives.[10] Neither would a Soviet attack in this region in itself provide an automatic escalation across the nuclear threshold. In areas of sparse population the damage and casualties could be limited and the combat maintained at a conventional phase. By the same token casualties sustained by elements of Ace Mobile, (e.g. a British Marine Commando) would not warrant a nuclear response, or even a counter on the Central Front. Perhaps the destruction of a Western capital ship such as an American aircraft carrier, with all its symbolic importance, could produce a Western retaliatory response, but presumably the Russians would be aware of this and so would avoid such temptation. If the West was able to deploy Atomic Demolition Mines (ADMs) in the path of the Soviet advance then it could provide an effective screen behind which the Allied forces could be deployed and reinforced. Such a strategem would confront the Russians with the agonizing dilemma of halting their own advance or moving ahead and therefore crossing the nuclear threshold; nor would there be a counter open to them which could be limited to the Northern flank and which would not be escalatory.

The NATO doctrine of 'flexible response' is not well adapted to the Northern flank of the Alliance. This is the problem of a big alliance trying to implement uniform standards without any regard for regional variations. There are more than a million Russians living within the environs of Murmansk so the Americans will not initiate any nuclear strike. In any case the Americans are unlikely to escalate across the nuclear threshold for an area which, in politico-strategic terms, is certainly not worth a nuclear war or a general conflict.

Despite these rather gloomy prognostications it is quite reasonable to maintain that under normal conditions the degree of vigilance maintained by the Norwegian forces deployed in Finnmark is such as to give sufficient warning of any Soviet build-up of forces which they would need to secure Allied territory. Soviet forces are seen as sufficient for the defence of their base and its environs and could provide the locus for a rapid reinforcement, over a period of time, should the need occur.

As we have seen the defence of Northern Norway is dependent upon the speedy movement of local, mobilized troops from the populous southern part of the country, together with the rapid influx of Allied reinforcements from key members of the Alliance.[11] In terms of the latter much will depend upon the ability of the Western navies to protect and convoy the reinforcements through the Norwegian Sea to the Northern ports. This accounts for the strategic importance of Iceland to NATO and in particular to Norway. Although Iceland supplies no armed forces to the Alliance its importance and contribution is centred on the Keflavik[12] airfield, which is the subject of a bilateral agreement with the United States. The American presence has been a source of domestic storm in Icelandic politics since the early days of the Cold War, and has been deeply resented by the local Communist Party.

Recently the seaward extension of Iceland's coastal boundaries was accepted, with varying degrees of grace, by all the nations whose trawlers fished those rich waters, except Great Britain. The action taken by Icelandic gunboats against British trawlers caught poaching, received a wide measure of popular support which cut across local political boundaries, as did the anger and resentment at the appearance of the Royal Navy. For the population of Iceland it was beyond their comprehension that their British allies could send in warships to coerce them by military force to yield on issues which the Icelanders regarded as vital to their economic survival. There was little real sympathy for Britain and the tactics of the Royal Navy came in for major censure from the NATO partners. As a consequence of British action support for NATO in Iceland was, for a while at least, severely circumscribed and for this reason the Americans and the Norwegians sought a speedy end to the Cod War. It is now quite clear that had the dispute been allowed to continue the result could have been a decision by the Iceland cabinet to re-examine its commitments and role in the North Atlantic Alliance. A hasty truce with Britain has for the present papered over the differences, but it is no more than a truce, and unless a more permanent solution can be found then the Cod War could break out again, but if it did it would be on a more vicious scale. It would only need a collision between a frigate and gunboat to produce a fatality for the crisis to deepen into a major confrontation between the two powers with the repercussions felt in the Alliance. Should Iceland either expel the Americans and/or leave NATO it would not automatically mean the Russians marching in, however much they desire it. Nevertheless the fact is that even without Russian presence a neutral Iceland would become another 'grey area' and thus add to the uncertainty and feed upon the instabilities which are present in the Northern flank. If there were a crisis in Finnmark the speedy movement of Western Maritime Forces into the Norwegian Sea could be severely constrained by the lack of air cover which had hitherto been afforded from Iceland. If time was allowed for the Keflavik airbase to be re-activated before the Second US Fleet entered the disputed waters, then this must destroy the delicate timetable of responses upon which Norwegian defence of its Northern territories is calculated. Thus in the event of Iceland becoming a 'grey area' there is bound to be a re-examination by the Norwegians of the whole direction and emphasis of their defence policy. This could mean a major revision of the Base Policy and the vexed issues surrounding the deployment and stationing of foreign troops on Norwegian soil.[13]

Given the build-up and forward deployment of the Soviet Northern Fleet into the North Atlantic, the position of Iceland assumes a critical importance in the super power balance. The Keflavik operation, from an American standpoint, is not crucial since it could be transferred to an airfield in Greenland. However, if the Russians were to acquire Keflavik then they could extend the zone of operations of the Northern Fleet secured by an air umbrella and for this reason the United States see Icelandic membership as vital to NATO. Hence in a future situation where Iceland was neutral, a super power crisis could in itself spark off a race for Iceland which could propel the two maritime powers into a war.

It would not be the first time in history that a neutral, but strategically desirable, piece of territory had acted as a catalyst between two contending great powers.

The Soviet Maritime presence in the Atlantic and North Sea is complemented to a certain degree by those warships stationed in the Baltic. This fleet is a considerable force but it does include an unusually large number of older warships which are used essentially in a training role. Together with the navies of Poland and the German Democratic Republic there is a heavy emphasis on amphibious warfare in the Baltic Sea.[14] For those major Soviet surface units and submarines that are destined to operate on the high seas, the narrow exits of the Baltic via the Danish straits are a major constraint. So hampered are the Russians by geography that they have recently sought another way out of these confined waters by constructing and extending the canal and river network that links the Baltic with the White Sea. However, should the Soviet Union seek to open up and secure the Baltic bottleneck then, in theory, there are two avenues of approach they could take: either an amphibious assault on the Danish Islands or a land advance through Schleswig-Holstein and then secure the islands from the Jutland peninsula. In more precise military terms either operation would also require the Soviet Union to mount a simultaneous assault on Southern Norway involving a belt of territory from Bergen to the Oslo Fjord if only to secure the Northern shore. Although the Warsaw Pact divisions stationed along the Baltic are strong there is a critical shortage of amphibious forces and there is little chance of this operation succeeding without giving some warning to the ever alert Norwegians. A NATO response to Soviet aggression to either Denmark or Norway is bound to be of a more virulent form than a response to a smash-and-grab raid in the North. A Soviet move in the Baltic approaches could not be launched in such a low profile and in so obvious a political vacuum so as not to warrant rapid movement through the threshold of nuclear retaliation by one side or the other. Contemporary international politics are becoming increasingly less and less predictable, but even so there would have to be a drastic shift in the central balance of power, and the whole nature of East-West relations would have to undergo traumatic revision before such an event as this would be in the remotest sense plausible.

An essential ingredient which confronts the Red Fleet in the Nordic balance is the position of Sweden and her powerful Navy.

Sweden has a coastline stretching for 2,700 kilometers from Southern Norway, where it dominates the Baltic bottleneck, to the Northern reaches of the Gulf of Bothnia and the border with Finland. Sweden is a traditional maritime state well used to operating naval squadrons in the confined waters of this inland sea. Throughout the Twentieth Century the navy has complemented the national government policy of non-alignment in peace and neutrality in war. For the navy the defence zone covers the entire extent of the Baltic to the enemy coast, and provides a first line of defence with submarines and Air Force strike squadrons. Swedish submarines are modern ships specifically built to meet the operational stringencies of a Baltic deployment. They are armed with homing torpedoes, have a mine-laying capability, and operate from a number of nuclear shelters hewn out of the mountainous coastline. The second line of defence consists of the fast gunboats backed up by larger surface units to destroyer size.[15] The Swedish navy pioneered the development and deployment of anti-ship missiles. At present the latest generation of Fast Patrol Boats (FPBs) are armed with the Norwegian produced Penguin missile. This underlines another development in naval affairs in this region with the three Scandinavian powers rationalizing their efforts in ships and weapons.[16] Any major Soviet or Pact aggression in the Baltic would produce a concerted joint operation by the Scandinavians.

Close inshore the Swedish navy has developed a quick reaction mine-laying capability which is dove-tailed into a regional defence mechanism. The latter is an intricate system of fixed and fortified installations equipped with long-range artillery, heavily protected rapid fire batteries and missile sites.[17] Taken in conjunction with NATO capabilities, and including those warships which the Federal Republic would deploy in the Baltic, it is clear that the Soviet Union face constraints of a different quality to those in the North Cape.

Both the Baltic and Kola bases provide the major Soviet naval presence for the North Atlantic and it is to this area of deployment that we should now direct our attention. In 1968 the Red Fleet carried out a major exercise,[18] which demonstrated their capability for sustained operations with larger forces at sea and exercised the co-operation between the Baltic and Northern Fleets. It was a forerunner for the multi-ocean exercise *Okean* in April 1970,[19] and there has since been a similar exercise on a global scale in April 1975.

Exercises of this nature gave the Soviet Fleet much needed

practice in the tasks of sustaining an operational deployment in the turbulent waters of the Atlantic. In terms of Western Forces the Soviet warships are confronted by the powerful United States Second Fleet,[20] comprising four strike-carriers and sixty surface combatants. Besides contributing to the nuclear-strike forces, these warships present a formidable array of naval talents from the most advanced techniques in ASW to amphibious assault. In addition the Royal Navy with its four Polaris submarines and the French with their three similar ships and their surface units, combine with the Americans to secure the Atlantic for Western defence. The balance between East and West has recently swung more in favour of the Soviet Union with new ship construction in the West failing to keep pace with the pensioning-off of older ships. Nevertheless this balance is somewhat restored when one considers the constraints under which the Soviet fleet has to operate. Passive sonar defences along the Atlantic seaboard of the United States, Western air superiority, and a multiple choice in base facilities, coupled with passage time for Soviet ships, are daunting limitations on operational efficiency.

It is vital that the sealanes across the Atlantic to the European theatres are maintained by the Western Alliance. One, however, would see this concept more in the political sense of Alliance solidarity at the present. It is clearly a prime mission of the Soviet navy in peacetime to publicize a presence in hitherto safe waters and thus help to engender a degree of uncertainty and doubt amongst the member states of the Western Alliance. In a sense the Russians are trying, by means of fleet activity, to influence Western public opinion and try and create a general awareness and perception of a Soviet presence. In a tactical sense the Western lead in ASW is a vital feature of the Atlantic but this is seen in terms of countering the Soviet SLBMs rather than escorting convoys in the mode of the Second World War. It would require a major conflict in the central front to be waged for a minimum of ninety days before the resources of Western powers would need revitalising through the convoying of merchant ships. Thus it is very hard to imagine a conflict of that duration remaining sub-critical in either the nuclear sense or that of territory. Nevertheless naval power in terms of professional expertise is indivisible and traditional maritime nations have to maintain an all-round capability and competence. Any concept based around a broken-backed war at sea has little relevance in the world of today, but a whole host of conditions and circumstances could arise in the future where such a prospect could be resurrected. In such an uncertain world situation, navies cannot suddenly rediscover lost techniques which might have been discarded at a previous time, and the lessons of the past do point to the essential dictum that seapower is indivisible.

The physical limitations under which the Soviet fleet has to operate in the 1970s have driven the Kremlin to seek short-term solutions to their problems. Narrow exits or choke-points, and long passages to patrol lines are vital considerations which caused the Russians to return to the scene of an earlier debâcle in the Caribbean. The first major Soviet naval squadron reappeared in these waters in June 1969 when a submarine tender, accompanied by two diesel-electric submarines and a *November* class nuclear vessel, arrived from the Kola Inlet. En route the force rendezvoused off the Azores with a *Kynda* class cruiser, a destroyer and frigate from the Black Sea Fleet. After refuelling from two naval auxiliaries the combined squadron steamed into the Caribbean under the watchful eyes of shadowing American forces. This operation was later appreciated as a blue print and test run for the more ambitious *Exercise Okean* of the following year. As part of the exercise a composite squadron of cruisers, cruise-missile submarines, and attendant auxiliaries entered the Cuban port of Cienfuegos, which in former days had been a port-of-call for American submarines. A *Tupolev 20 Bear* long-range maritime patrol aircraft flew 5,000 miles from the Kola Inlet to an airfield in Cuba as part of the same operation. *Exercise Okean* did present the Soviet Navy with the opportunity of demonstrating its multi-ocean capability in operations of this type, although the impact was somewhat nullified by the unfortunate foundering of a *November* class submarine in the South-West approaches to Britain in full view of Western shadowing forces.

The advantages to the Soviet Union of a base to support missile submarines in Cuba was obvious, and not least of which is that the time saved in transit from Northern waters can be utilized in longer patrol on station off the Atlantic seaboard. In a fairly obvious manner, Soviet intentions in Cienfuegos became apparent when an *Alligator* class landing ship accompanied by a submarine tender, a missile cruiser and a destroyer arrived in the port later that year. Barges were unloaded and work undertaken in the construction of shore facilities, despite a pointed and public warning from the United States Government.

Since *Exercise Okean* a Caribbean presence has become a fact of life for the Soviet navy, whose warships monitor traffic using the Panama Canal, maintain a discreet watch over American naval exercises, and keep a watching brief on the Atlantic missile test range.

Finally, it is worth turning our attention to more immediate concerns by examining Soviet naval activity in the North Sea and UK home waters. There has been some speculation in the Western Press in recent months over the political dynamite they envisage being created by a combustible combination of 'the red fleet and black gold'. There has been considerable Soviet naval activity in this area for a variety of reasons of which very little is connected with oil exploration. Russian ships as a major commitment concentrate instead on American Polaris activity in Holy Loch and the Royal Navy in Rosyth. Other naval activity can be explained by the normal access traffic moving from the Atlantic into the Baltic Sea, while other ships, in particular AGIs, have monitored the British missile range in the Orkney Islands.

From a British viewpoint we are discussing the North Sea as an 'offshore tapestry', an inter-related matrix of peace-time responsibilities for the Royal Navy. Such tasks include fishery protection, where Russian trawlers are a problem, service and assistance to the capital investment of energy installations, and environmental protection and pollution controls.[21] Soviet warships and AGIs have shown interest in the off-shore installations and they are also complicating factors by injecting an air of uncertainty into very expensive operations. It is more likely, however, that these Soviet ships, in keeping with Russian policy elsewhere, are probably monitoring Western techniques for their own needs. Because of the unequivocal British sovereignty[22] exercised over the exploration of the Continental Shelf, the activities of the Soviet Navy, barring accidents or poor seamanship, do not present a threat.

Thus, for the Soviet Union the location of its base complexes in the Kola Inlet and the Baltic Sea, and the resultant strain this imposes on transit routes are major constraints on operations in the North Atlantic. There is little doubt that for the present the Soviet naval strength in these Northern waters is more than sufficient to defend Russia's vital interests. But geography fatally inhibits any would-be Soviet ambitions to achieve more, such as creating a controlling presence in the vital areas of the mid-Atlantic. Beside a considerably expanded ship capability, it would require the prior destruction, occupation or at least neutralization of considerable areas of NATO territory including Northern Norway, Denmark,

Iceland and even the outer island chain of the United Kingdom. This would mean a scale of operations that would quickly lead to a major escalation in the Western response. The close linkage between the maritime environment of the North Atlantic, the Central European Fronts, and the overall strategic nuclear posture is the indisputable strength of the Alliance.

Therefore NATO commands the high ground and looks down on the Soviet Union and nothing short of a determined Soviet offensive is going to reverse the essential constraints of geography. In these circumstances the most likely use of Soviet naval power is indirect and in peacetime aims to create an impact on the public mind of the Western World. It is quite possible that an increased presence of warships, and the frequent sightings and faithful reporting by the Press of new impressive surface units of the Red Fleet, can become a received idea to the public at large, as well as causing an unsettled effect in political circles. The media, who have a duty and an inalienable right to report the facts, do little of service to the Alliance, and perform a valuable function for the Soviet Navy when such information is embroidered for the sake of a newsworthy item, beyond the real capability of the fleet. Alarmist, rather than realist reporting simply enhances the threat of the Soviet navy to the integrity of the Western World.

Notes

1. The Denmark Straits have figured in a number of prominent naval actions of the recent past, the most famous of which was the sinking of the *Hood* by the *Bismarck* in May 1941.

2. The standing forces of the Norwegian Army are concentrated in the counties of Troms and Finnmark. There are two small garrisons in Finnmark: 450 men at Kirkenes and a battalion group of 1,000 men at Lakselu-Banak. The stationing of combat forces from NATO allies in Norway is clearly prescribed in the diplomatic note sent to Moscow in February 1949. This has since become known as the 'base policy' which controls the movement and duration of Allied exercises on Norwegian soil and the 'peacetime' visits of allied warships. Since 1949 the Base Policy has defined 'permissible activity' to include Norwegian participation in NATO HQs and infrastructure, the stationing of Allied officers at HQAFNORTH at Kolsas (near Oslo); Norwegian involvement in exercises with ACE Mobile Force; the construction and operation of early-warning systems. In 1961 in a further exchange of notes the Norwegians declared a prohibition on the deployment of nuclear weapons in Norwegian territory.

3. It is worth remembering that the Kola Inlet is not just an isolated fjord containing a naval base. The Soviet Union has developed the area as an industrial complex in its own right. The Kola Peninsula has an urban population in excess of 800,000 people and amongst its industrial activities phosphate, fertilizers, and alloy metals figure prominently. The region supports more than 400 trawlers, has two nuclear power stations and will undoubtedly be an important centre for future oil exploitation of the Barents Sea. The Soviet stake in the Kola Peninsula in economic as well as strategic terms is quite significant.

4. In particular the writings of Johan Jørgen Holst. A book which he edited entitled *Five Roads to Nordic Security*, published in 1973 by Universitetsforlaget of Oslo, examines this whole question in great detail.

5. The original treaty which recognized Norwegian sovereignty of the Svalbard Archipelago was signed in 1920 and the Soviet Union acceded to the Treaty in 1935. For a full account of Soviet/Norwegian relations and interests in Svalbard see Johan Hølst *Five Roads to Nordic Security* footnote 4 Ibid pages 109-113.

6. Soviet sensitivities in this region were seen as linked to the strange circumstances involving the loss of the British Trawler *Gaul* in 1975.

7. It would not be difficult to attach some monitoring device or even a sonar to an oil platform.

8. Lecture given in Oslo in 1975.

9. Northern Norway comes under the responsibility of Saclant and in any crisis the build-up of reinforcements would follow a clearly laid contingency plan.

10. The Norwegians have come under some considerable pressure from the Western Alliance to revise some of the more restrictive aspects of the Base Policy to take account of the much increased Soviet presence in the Northern region. There seems little evidence that the Stortig will relent.

11. Key members in this instance would point to United States, Canada and the United Kingdom. Recent reviews of British defence have led to a withdrawal from the Mediterranean and a heavier commitment to the Northern Flank.

12. In practice the United States has two bases in Iceland. Besides Keflavik in the South there is a radar station in the South-Eastern tip of Iceland at Hornafjordur. The Keflavik airfield is a US Navy responsibility which deploys a squadron of *F102 Interceptors* for local defence, a squadron of *P.3c Orion* long-range maritime reconnaissance aircraft, and a flight of *EC-181 airborne* early warning aircraft. There are about 3,500 servicemen stationed in Iceland.

13. Icelandic neutrality might be all that is required for the Norwegians to accept the deployment of tactical nuclear weapons in their territory and a more permanent presence of foreign troops.

14. The Polish Army includes an amphibious assault division and both Navies have a significant number of landing ships. The Polish Navy has 23 *Polnochy* class landing craft, and the German Democratic Republic 6 *Robbe* class

and 12 *Labo* class landing craft. This is enough for limited scale operations such as the seizure of an island but not enough for any major offensive.

15. Janes accredit the Swedish Navy with 8 destroyers, 5 frigates, 22 submarines.

16. The sixteen ships of the *Jagaren* class of Fast Attack Craft are modelled on the Norwegian *Snogg* class (lead ship was built in Norway). The Danes built four minelayers of the *Falster* class to Scandinavian/NATO design.

17. The Swedish and Norwegian Coastal Artillery Services are very similar. They both represent separate branches of the navy, are organized on the basis of gun batteries, torpedo batteries and controlled minefields. The Norwegians have deployed sixteen Swedish 75 mm Bofors automatic coastal guns.

18. Exercise Sever was followed up by a Spring exercise in 1969 when twenty warships were deployed in the Southern Norwegian Sea. Exercise Sever, however, concentrated on amphibious operations and a landing task-force of five destroyers and five landing ships assembled off the coast of Southern Norway and sailed north to practise opposed landings in the Kola area.

19. Exercise Okean produced the largest ever concentration of Soviet warships in the Norwegian Sea, with eighty vessels deployed. There was a second amphibious exercise with the force coming in from the Baltic, supported this time by a helicopter carrier and exercised on the Rybachi Peninsula.

20. US Second Fleet would form part of the Maritime Contingency Force Atlantic (Marconforlant) consisting of Striking Fleet Atlantic (two carrier-strike groups, one American and one Anglo-Dutch) and an Amphibious Force of Marines from United States, Britain, and the Netherlands.

21. For which purpose a new class of 16-knot fishery protection boats of 1,000 tons have been ordered from the Royal Navy. They are affectionately known as the 'North Sea Pandas.'

22. In 1964 the United Kingdom passed the Continental Shelf Act whereby offences on the installations on the UK Continental Shelf are treated as though they occurred in Britain itself.

CHAPTER NINE

The Soviet Fleet and the Indian Ocean

Of all the seas which have witnessed the activities of the Soviet Navy in recent years, the Indian Ocean is the most enigmatic when it comes to divining motives and objectives. In the absence of empirical evidence, comment has to be largely a matter of conjecture, although in other seas and oceans evidence of capabilities and objectives is somewhat easier to interpret. Hitherto the answer given by the media to a Soviet presence in the Indian Ocean, that it is the same as all the other oceans because the Americans are there with *Polaris* submarines, does not really stand up to close examination. The Press in particular have always focused a lot of attention on Soviet activities in the Indian Ocean out of all proportion to their actual physical presence; the result has been to confuse an already complicated picture. In this chapter I hope to unravel some of the mysteries surrounding the role of the navies of both super powers in the Indian Ocean and to examine in some detail the available evidence which can give a lead to the aspirations of Soviet maritime power.

For more than two centuries the Indian Ocean was the special domain of Great Britain and it was the White Ensign which proudly flew above sparkling quarter-decks in a hundred ports of call. The Indian Ocean is a vast expanse of water: from Fremantle in West Australia to the naval base at Colombo in Ceylon, (now Sri Lanka) which is approximately mid-point in the Ocean, is the same distance (3,000 miles) as Southampton to New York. Sailing north from Colombo to the one-time British protectorate of Aden, a distance of more than 2,000 miles, you have covered the length of the Mediterranean. As long as the British Empire controlled the Indian

Ocean, it could be regarded as a strategic entity. Control was assured by possession of those territories which dominated the entrances and exits to the Ocean and the Dominions and colonies among the littoral states. The picture was complete with Royal Navy cruisers patrolling a well-worn path along the major shipping routes which dissected the ocean in their task of protecting the national interests of the British Empire.

The demise of Great Britain caused a major shift in those factors which can exert a political and strategic interest in the area. In the first instance neither super power has been able to fill the vacuum left by the British, and secondly no littoral state has been able to project an ocean-wide maritime presence. In naval terms the area seems to be in a strange form of limbo; only three local states have shown any potential as naval powers and these, India, South Africa and Iran, are all at different stages of naval evolution, though none has appeared the exclusive client of one super power.[1] The remainder of the littoral states are all developing nations and most of them do not even posses sufficient naval power to protect their own coastal interests.

The Russians' main interest in the Indian Ocean was maritime as Russian freighters sailed in transit from home ports to Haiphong, carrying supplies for the North Vietnamese war efforts. By 1968 in addition to this mercantile factor, Soviet interests and attention had become focused on the Indian Ocean for a number of differing reasons. Without prejudging the issue with a list of priorities the Russians could not, as a developing great naval power, be unaffected by the debates and eventual decision taken by Britain to abandon an East-of-Suez role. Also, with the gradual strengthening and modernizing process of the navy in its main fleet bases, the problems of warships having to make the long haul between the Pacific base and European Waters by transit of the Indian Ocean, must have raised the intriguing question of securing base facilities to relieve the strain of such a long voyage. Thirdly, by the year 1968 the Soviet rupture with China was assuming an increasingly menacing and hostile form.

The Soviet Union saw the need to develop a policy which in a rather crude manner aimed at containing any possible Chinese ambitions in Southern Asia and the isolation of China politically through a policy of encirclement. This brought the Russians into closer contact with the government of India, where a measure of common ground and harmony was found on a number of issues.

India had reason to fear what it perceived as the acquisitive tendencies of Chinese ambitions in Southern Asia, and in the earlier sixties her armed forces had been mauled and humiliated by the Chinese Army in the Himalayan frontier regions. Another area which they had in common was that India was in the market for a new navy. In the war with Pakistan in 1965 the Indian navy had performed tolerably well but its ships, of British origin, were Second World War vintage[2] and beginning to show their age. In the unfinished business engendered by the indecisiveness of the Pakistan clash, the Indian government felt obliged to modernize the navy before the next round of the struggle with their Moslem rival. The British and Americans had placed an arms embargo on India as a result of the war with Pakistan so the Soviet Union, which had already established an influence through its mediation in the Treaty of Tashkent, stood by to make good the Indian naval deficit. Over the next couple of years the Soviet Union provided India with six modern escorts[3] and a flotilla of *O*sa class missile gunboats. In addition the Indian Navy was, for the first time, able to develop a sub-surface capability with Russian supplied *Foxtrot* class submarines. Another gap in the Indian Naval expertise was rectified by the provision of amphibious warfare ships and landing craft. In return the Indian government leased port facilities to the Russians at Vishakhapatnam[4] which the latter proceeded to modernize and extend into a submarine base. Activities such as these were accompanied by frequent naval visits to Bombay, Madras and the availability of naval facilities in the Andaman Islands.[5] It came as no surprise to Western analysts when the Treaty of Friendship and Co-operation was signed between the two states in 1971. India had thus under the skilled leadership of Nehru pioneered the concept of non-alignment, carved out for herself a world role in the process, and within a few years of Nehru's death become Russia's closest ally outside Europe.

Important as the naval connection with India was in the Soviet grand strategy against China it was an expensive programme and not of vital interest to the security of the Soviet Union. Instead we find the clue to Soviet interests in an initiative launched earlier in 1964 in the United Nations when they proposed that the Indian Ocean should become a nuclear-free zone. At that time Russian analysts were becoming aware and increasingly alarmed by the Americans' development of the longer ranged and more powerful *Polaris A3* strategic missile. This focused their attention on possible waters from which such warheads could be launched on the Soviet Union from patrolling submarines. The Arabian Sea and the North-West quadrant of the Indian Ocean Basin were seen to offer to the Americans the alluring prospect of a whole series of targets in Southern Russia and also parts of China. Given the distance from Soviet bases in the Black Sea and the Pacific it must have appeared to be a more cost effective objective to secure a ban on super power naval activity in that area than to try to counter an American presence with Soviet warships. When the diplomatic initiative failed, the Russians attempted to secure a presence in these now vital waters before any American move to take up another option in their global strategy of a seaborne-secure second strike. It certainly looked at the time as if the Americans were seriously considering the Northern waters of the Indian Ocean as an area for *Polaris* patrols. In 1966 the British and Americans reached agreement over the British Indian Ocean Territory as an area for the joint development of base facilities while in North-West Cape, Australia, the US Navy was constructing a VLF radio communication complex of the type required to direct and control *Polaris* missions.

Although the North-West quadrant of the Indian Ocean Basin does allow the largest coverage of Soviet territory by a 3,000 mile range missile system of any sea, there is no published evidence that the Americans have ever exercised this option in any major fashion to date. The reasons for this are fairly straightforward: the United States Navy has a secure second strike capability and also the passage of Polaris submarines from their bases in Holy Loch, Rota, or Guam is so far that there would be little time for actual patrol within the limits set by a normal sixty day mission. Nevertheless Soviet perceptions of possible American options conditioned a move into this area, and since the later sixties the Russians have secured a measure of influence in the littoral states of the Horn of Africa with the leasing of port facilities in Berbera and the military sponsorship of the Somali Republic.[6] Across the narrow waters of the Dab El Mandeb Straits Soviet warships have been frequent visitors to the port of Aden since the demise of the British.[7]

The polar projectory of the Soviet space programme passes over the Indian Ocean from the northern tip of the Malagasy Republic to the Arabian Sea and there have been as many as twenty Soviet ships, tenders, freighters, telemetry vessels[8] and survey ships on station in these waters in support of various space programmes and, on occasion, capsules have been recovered.

As the north-west quadrant shows us, the process of establishing a Soviet presence and influence in the Indian Ocean is the result of a whole series of trends and decisions which have been taken in conjunction with a complex matrix of economic and political as well as military and strategic factors. There seems little doubt that the Indian Ocean presence reflected some of the domestic pressures on Admiral Gorshkov and the naval lobby inside the Kremlin and the hierarchy of the Communist Party machine. From what is known in the West of some of the in-fighting within the Soviet Union, Gorshkov has had to struggle for funds to build new and expensive ships often against the entrenched opposition of the Army and Air Force. Thus the entry of the Soviet Navy in to the Indian Ocean, virgin waters from a naval standpoint, could be partly seen in terms of the response to domestic pressure.

A further area of Soviet maritime interest in the Indian Ocean has been the much publicised activity of its fishing fleets. The Russians are about third in the world league of fishing nations, and this reflects the importance of fish as a protein to make up the short fall in the grain harvest. The Soviet Union, however, is a long way from the best fishing grounds in the world and so it has developed an advanced technology in distant water operations.[9] This has involved the deployment of large factory refrigeration ships[10] together with their attendant trawlers. Despite the clamourings of the Western Press, the vast majority of Russian trawlers are just that and everyone of them is needed to provide food for domestic consumption. It so happens that the Soviet spy-ships or intelligence gatherers (AGI) are constructed on the same basic hull design of the multi-purpose *Elint* class trawlers.[11] To the trained observer the intelligence ship with its forest of aerials and electronic gadgetry is clearly discernible for what it is, and there is no published evidence to suggest that such a role is clandestinely moved into the more innocent trawler activity. For a number of years the Soviet Union has been fishing the rich and abundant waters off the South African coast, in what has become a highly sophisticated and co-ordinated operation which has paid little heed to the needs of environmental control or protection of the species. In order to improve the efficiency of this operation, the trawlers have been using the port of Aden for a number of years for repair, and the Russians have been allowed to maintain a small team of marine engineers there for that purpose. In 1970 the Soviet Union concluded an agreement with the small and independent island republic of Mauritius whereby Aeroflot could fly out from the Soviet Union relief crews to a specially enlarged airfield. This, of course, makes sound common sense for the Soviet Union since it does allow the trawlers to remain on station and the crews to be rotated on a regular, though by the Mauritians, strictly controlled basis.[12]

Thus by the early seventies the pattern of the Soviet Naval presence in the Indian Ocean had clearly emerged. After the closure of the Suez Canal in 1967 the bulk of the visiting ships were provided by the Pacific Fleet in Vladivostock though occasionally a small force would make the voyage from the Northern Fleet. The composition of the force was invariably small and followed a pretty regular format. The lead ship is a cruiser and is accompanied by a couple of destroyers, and support ships together with two submarines. This main force sails from Vladivostock before the onset of the Russian winter and enters the Indian Ocean in December. This force will exercise and make a number of courtesy visits before returning to its home base usually in May or June; it is relieved by a smaller force of usually two destroyers and attendant supply ships. In between official visits and the occasional exercise, these Russian squadrons spend a fair amount of their time at anchorage. To this end the Soviet Navy have laid permanent anchorages and mooring buoys some 250 nm East of Durban and 150 nm South-West of Malagasy. There are other anchorages off the Seychelles, Socotra, the Maldive Islands, and the Chagos Archipelagos, and the warships are reported to refuel from tankers lying at anchor in the Mozambique Channel.[13]

While an increasing number of Soviet crews have become familiar with the long cruises of the Indian Ocean and the officers gained invaluable experience, the fleet in itself has contributed to a projection of power ashore and has exerted some influence over events. Albeit in indirect manner, the presence of a Soviet squadron can lend diplomatic respectability and thus political stability to a government under pressure. An often quoted example was the prolonged stay by two destroyers in Mogadiscio in 1969, at a time when the government of the Somali Republic was threatened by unrest and revolt.

After the Mediterranean, the Indian Ocean has figured highest in terms of good-will visits by units of the Soviet fleet and this feature has been interpreted by one school of Western opinion in a most sinister manner, as a threat to Western commerce and interests. For this extreme point of view the Soviet presence in the Arabian Sea and the Mozambique Channel, in particular, represents an attempt by the Soviet Union to be able to cut off Western oil supplies should the need arise.[14] As if to lend force to the debate, this opinion cites the historical precedent of the combined U-Boat and Commerce Raider Campaigns launched by the Germans during World War Two and the need to retain Simonstown as a Western naval base.

In the first instance the Russians are hardly likely to interfere in the movement of Western oil supplies, for besides provoking the Americans with an immediate counter, it would hardly please the Arab producers who are increasingly dependent upon the revenue they earn from the export of their oil. Throughout the short history of their maritime presence the Soviet Union have taken great care not to arouse the susceptibilities of the littoral states by any intrusive display of their maritime power. Secondly, the Cape route is often mistakenly described as a bottleneck. There is a concentration of shipping in what is in reality a very wide channel and this is caused by ships deliberately 'cutting the corner' to save on transit time and thus reduce costs in transportation. In practice it would be exceedingly difficult for any navy to effectively police the area and prohibit the movement of traffic. Finally, to embark on any strategy which involved the physical disruption of shipping, the Russians would require a major deployment of surface vessels, which would need a major base in the vicinity rather than the base facilities which they have at present. There is little doubt that any sinking of Western ships by submarines or surface craft would produce an immediate response and escalation by the Western World. It is also worth remembering that with the ever increasing tonnage of the Russian mercantile marine plying the trade routes, they are equally vulnerable, and have a vested interest in the uninhibited passage of the high seas.

The naval presence of the super powers in the Indian Ocean, though still small has increased in numbers and quality over the years and it is the novelty, pace, size, and also visibility of this process which has aroused the attention of the Western Press and the fears of the littoral states.[15] Each super power, primarily there to provide an alternative to the growth in influence of the other, is also aware of the opportunities that abound in this region for the deployment of naval forces as flexible and physical extensions of state diplomacy. Two examples of such activity, the Commonwealth Prime Ministers Conference in 1971 and the naval manoeuvring which accompanied the Indo-Pakistan War of 1971, are worthy of further scrutiny.

In January 1971 the Commonwealth Prime Ministers Conference was convened in Singapore and although as is usual on these occasions, a number of subjects were under discussion, most attention was focussed on the publically declared intention of the British Prime Minister, Edward Heath, to re-open the Arms trade with South Africa. This decision reflected the growing fears of the new British government about the increased Soviet naval activities, and was directly related to the decision to expand the base facilities at the South African port of Simonstown. This initiative aroused the fury and wrath of many of the Black African leaders when at the peak of the controversy and almost precisely on cue, two Soviet warships, a large cruiser and a destroyer[16], sailed by within sight of the Singapore shore. This force was immediately followed by an AGI which quite blatantly loitered in the Man-of-War Passage and presumably monitored the diplomatic traffic emanating out of the Singapore Conference.

Ever since this strange event Western commentators have argued over the reasons that could possibly have prompted the Russians to seemingly lend weight to Heath's case by appearing in awesome might a mile off-shore on cue! Never before in the history of international diplomacy has a statesman been presented with the means to stage-manage effects to lend such force to his argument. One school of thought has produced a thesis which suggests that the ships would have reinforced the Heath case amongst those Commonwealth states who would have the most reason to fear a Soviet presence and thus desire Britain to retain Simonstown. These states would include the white Australians and New Zealanders and, so the argument goes, would drive a deep wedge between the White States and Black powers who in any case had nothing to fear from a Soviet maritime presence. If this is the case it does show a most intriguing use of seapower as an instrument of statecraft, and for it to be true would also have required the Russians to have had precise knowledge of Prime Minister Heath's speech! It is more likely that *Mr Heath* had the precise information on Soviet naval movements—Royal Navy warships were presumably shadowing the Russian units—and *he* was able to use this information. The whole episode thus seems to have been a miscalculation or oversight on the part of the Soviet Union. A voyage of this distance and duration would take some months to arrange from Vladivostok, and probably the initial decisions on departure dates and course were taken when Mr Wilson was the Prime Minister and the South African question not an issue worthy of consideration. Subsequent events can, I believe, be reasonably explained by a failure in communication and lack of coordination between the naval planners and the political overlords. In a system such as that which prevails in the Soviet Union, which is heavily bureaucratic, it would not be an unusual occurrence. Nevertheless the political gaffe must have caused some considerable embarrassment to the Kremlin, and senior naval officers at Vladivostock presumably came in for severe censure.

By the autumn of the same year the breakdown in authority in East Pakistan, together with the repressive measures of the Central Government, had spawned a secessionist movement which, in turn, caused a deterioration in relations between Pakistan and India. Events moved quickly and when the movement of refugees became an intolerable flood the Indian Armed Forces, in a brilliantly planned and well-executed operation, invaded East Pakistan in the name of the secessionist cause.[17] In December 1971, at the height of the conflict, the major foreign navy was a Royal Navy task group. The squadron which comprised the attack, Carrier *Eagle* and the Commando Carrier *Albion* together with their attendant escorts and RFA supply ships, covered the withdrawal of the British Forces in the Persian Gulf. Their role ostensibly was to insure that, in a rather unsettling time, the final vestiges of the British presence could be withdrawn peacefully and to deter any local power from taking advantage of the situation.[18]

At that time of year, the Soviet presence was a nominal force of two destroyers who were awaiting relief by the more powerful group that seasonally appeared at that time. The latter which had left Vladivostock some weeks earlier, comprised a missile cruiser and *Juliet* class submarines, and reinforced the original force. The emphasis in cruise missiles in the combined Soviet group suggested that the Russians saw this as a counter to the carrier task force of the Royal Navy already stationed in the India Ocean. The United States in the meanwhile responded by withdrawing units of the Seventh Fleet on duty off Vietnam[19] and forming a task group which they called Taskforce 74. On the 14th December this taskforce led by the *USS Enterprise* and the helicopter carrier *Tripoli* together with guided missile armed escorts, and a nuclear-powered attack submarine, was despatched into the Indian Ocean 'to protect US interests' in the area.

A build-up of super power naval presence now continued with the dispatch of a second Soviet group, presumably in response to Task Force 74 from Vladivostok. This time the Russian units comprised a *Kresta* cruiser, a *Kashin* class destroyer[20], two submarines and supply ships. By the end of the month the Americans had fourteen ships, the Russians twenty-six and the British seventeen on station in the Indian Ocean. From the standpoint of seapower the Indo-Pakistan War presents us with an interesting situation, for besides the sheer numbers, it is the first time it was possible to witness the presence of both powers in strength. It is not unusual for a Western naval force in distant waters to respond to a local crisis, but it was an entirely new experience for them to have to take account of the Russian naval presence. By the time the major protagonists arrived on the scene the war was over, and a ceasefire came into effect at the end of the month. The only warship which made any positive move was *HMS Albion* which steamed towards the Bay of Bengal as a contingency to rescue foreign nationals. In fact the need did not arise and the *Albion* quickly withdrew to the South to link up with her consorts in South African ports, where they spent Christmas and the New Year. By the same token Soviet motives and deployments can be easily explained. Their first task group, originally intended as a relief force, joined up with units already on station to provide an anti-carrier counter to the Royal Navy presence. Similarly the second group was hurriedly dispatched to balance Task Force 74 for again its composition was that of an anti-carrier group. Once they entered the Indian Ocean the Russian units moved off to shadow the Western units and would presumably have become hostile had any attempt been made to interfere in the war against the Soviet client state of India.

American motives and intentions are more difficult to fathom and one is left with the inescapable conclusion that it was a case of miscalculation and gross over-reaction. Relations between the United States and the Republic of India had never been close ever since the policies of Nehru and non-alignment had aroused the deep antagonism of Dulles. By the time that the United States had come to adopt a less extreme stance on Asian security, relations between the two states had become influenced by India's quarrel with the United States' allies, Cento and Seato, in Pakistan. From the outset of the crisis in 1971 the United States had sponsored the cause of Pakistan, first by seeking to discredit India in the Security Council of the United Nations, and then by re-equipping the Pakistan

Airforce with new machines flown in via Libya and Jordan. When these measures failed to correct the downward swing of Pakistani fortunes, it seemed an obvious escalation to reinforce American intentions by the move of powerful naval units into the area. American behaviour can also be explained by the imminence of the Peking summit and by their natural distaste for secessionist movements. Finally, the State Department considered that Bangladesh represented an unfortunate and potentially[21] destabilising precedent in Third World politics. This particular region abounded with new states founded on obscure and fragile nationalisms, and it was thus the American intention to see in Task Force 74 a strong visible presence from which such states could draw succour, and thus counter similar trends within their own frontiers.

Nevertheless the Indian Government saw in the American presence and the appearance of the *USS Enterprise* off the Bay of Bengal an unwarranted interference in their sovereign affairs. The Indians who neither sought nor needed Soviet support in their quarrel with Pakistan viewed the American intrusion in the light of the history of Indo-American relations. The United States Government came in for much adverse comment and criticism as a result of this escapade, and it is rather ironic to see both super states making such major miscalculations in the exercise of their seapower in the same ocean and within such a short space of time.

In terms of the future the Soviet Union has made it abundantly clear that it intends to deploy a maritime presence in the Indian Ocean which is commensurate with that of a power with global interests. This presence whilst fanning out across the ocean will emphasise the Arabian Sea and the Indian Ocean Basin for all the reasons I have discussed and because the Middle East represents an area of prime concern to security. In terms of more confined waters, such as the Red Sea and Persian Gulf, the opportunist and occasionally adventurist streak in Soviet foreign policy may well seek advantage through the deployment of seapower.[22] In this context perhaps the Russians will need to seek accommodation or take notice of the developing maritime capability of states like Iran and, to a lesser extent, Saudi Arabia. The United States for its part will maintain a limited interest and possibly develop some base facilities in strategically located islands,[23] and it is possible that the new *Trident* class FBMs will patrol in the Indian Ocean from the Guam base when they become operational. The British, for their part, will exercise in the area on occasion with task-forces en route to the Far East and Hong Kong.

The Soviet Navy has become then a force to be reckoned with and its confident deployments into distant waters is a cause for concern for local powers with naval aspirations such as Iran. As the Iranian navy also gains in strength and expertise it will presumably seek to challenge any Soviet attempt to fill the vacuum left by the British. At the same time the Iranians are bound to find strong local competition and rivalry from the Soviet-sponsored Indian Navy, which in itself presents an intriguing situation for the future. The whole region does contain the potential for inter-state conflicts, and regional instabilities are an incipient feature of this part of the world. The roles that the Soviet Navy may be called on to fulfil are difficult to ascertain with any precision except that the threat syndrome does seem to have a greater relevance for the littoral states than the Western world.

Notes

1. The Indian Navy has British warships and the more recent acquisitions are Soviet. South Africa has British with French-supplied submarines while Iran has British and American designs.

2. Thus, for instance, the Indian navy flagship was the *Delhi*, better and formerly known as HMS *Achilles*, a 6 in. gun-cruiser which fought at the Battle of the River Plate in 1939. The 11th Destroyer Squadron were ex-British R Class of the Second World War vintage. There were some more modern frigates of the British *Leopard*, *Whitney* and *Blackwood* class, but the remainder were *Hunts*, *Black Swan* and *River* class from the war years.

3. By 1974/5 the Soviet Union has equipped the Indian navy with:
   8 *Petya* class small frigates
   8 *Osa* class fast attack/missile boats
   8 *Foxtrot* class diesel submarines together with a modified *Ugra* class tender.
   The cruiser *Delhi* has been relegated to a training role and India is purchasing further frigates from France (A69 *Avisos*) and 6 British *Leander* class are to be built under licence.
   The amphibious warfare capability comes in the form of 4 *Polnocny* class delivered in 1966/8.

4. In the Bay of Bengal some 500 miles south of Calcutta.

5. Port Blaire in South Andaman.

6. Soviet-supplied equipment to the Somali Democratic Republic to date includes T/55 and BTR armoured vehicles, MiG-17 FGA, MiG 21 fighters while the navy has SO1-class submarines chasers and MTBs. What is disconcerting is the T-4 landing craft together with the AN-2 tactical transport

aircraft. In June 1975 American satellite photographs revealed Russian technicians building a Soviet missile storage and handling base at Berbera.

7. The navies of both the Yemen Arab Republic and Yemen: People's Democratic Republic (South Yemen) have been equipped by the Soviet Union with light craft.

8. Including the 45,000 ton *Kosmonaut Yuriy Gagarin*, the largest Soviet Space Associated ship.

9. For a more detailed account of Russian Fishery see the survey in I. P. Moskovoj, 'Soviet Sea-fisheries 1970–75', *Navy International*, June 1976.

10. The *Vostock* of 43,000 tons is a factory ship and trawler mother ship designed with the tropics in mind.

11. As Intelligence Gatherers (AGIs) the Elint hull is used by the *Okean*, *Lentra* and *Hayak* class. According to Janes there are fifty-three AGIs in the Soviet Navy.

12. The Agreement does not prohibit Soviet warships from visiting Mauritius and presumably making use of the trawlers' facilities.

13. It is reported in 1975 that the Russians are negotiating with Samora Machel, President of the Frelimo Government of Mozambique, for naval facilities at the Port of Nacala. The Soviet overtures were spurned by Peking orientated Mozambique.

14. 25 million tons of oil is transported around the Cape each month en route to Western Europe and the Americas.

15. The Cuban presence in Anglo, 12,000 military personnel and a vast supply of Russian equipment, has made the South Africans especially alarmed. Much of the equipment was carried in Russian, East German and Yugoslav freighters.

16. The *Sverdlov* class 6-inch gun armed cruiser *Alexander Suvorov* and the *Kotlin* class destroyer *Blestyashchiy*.

17. And the state of Bangladesh was born. This new state has a population of 75 million and this lends weight to the Indian Armed Forces claim that their operation was the largest liberation force since 1944.

18. The British fear was that in the uncertain atmosphere either one of the many dynastic quarrels would erupt or even worse that the Iranians might use the British withdrawal as a smokescreen to establish a presence on one of the disputed islands at the mouth of the Persian Gulf. This powerful naval squadron was intended to deter the Iranian navy from adventurism.

19. Withdrawn from Yankee station.

20. Emphasis again on a balanced counter to a carrier task group.

21. President Nixon's visit to Peking in February 1972 had obviously taken great care and diplomatic finesse to arrange and Dr. Kissinger was most concerned lest American reaction to the Indo-Pakistan War should undermine the initiative.

22. For the present the Russians have lost their influence in Iraq, who are looking Westward again. The Iranians have mended their forces with the Iraqis and seem, in co-operation with Great Britain, to be in the final

stages of the successful war against the Omani Rebels. The Americans maintain a small naval presence in the Gulf centred on Bahrain.

23. At various times the United States have been interested in both Nasirah Islands, just 400 miles from the strategically important Straits of Hormuz, and Diego Quarcia, 2,000 miles further into the Ocean and more centrally located to mount air surveillance of Soviet naval activities. An occasional carrier task group comes in from the Seventh Fleet. The new *Nimitz* class, 100,000 ton nuclear-powered attack carriers would be ideal for these long sorties but the lead ship, the newly commissioned *Nimitz*, is to make her first combat commission in the Mediterranean.

CHAPTER TEN

The Pacific Fleet

The geography of the Pacific Ocean and its littoral states is the geography of contrast and extremes. It is the world's largest ocean and occupies more of the surface of the earth than all the land masses added together. This huge expanse of water allowed the Japanese in 1941 to hide the movement of a strike fleet in its long voyage towards Pearl Harbour; and the Americans to retaliate later at the Battle of Midway,[1] by concealing from the Japanese the presence of their aircraft carriers. In contrast movement of shipping into the ocean can easily be registered and thus controlled, because of the dominating position of the Indonesian Archipelago and the scarcity of deep-water channels in the East,[2] and the economic convenience in the West afforded by the Panama Canal. Even so it is a long way across the Pacific, for example it is 10,000 miles north to south, from the Bering Sea to Antarctica, and it is a further 9,000 miles east to west, from the city state of Singapore to the Panama Canal. The littoral states of the Pacific Ocean include the two most powerful in the United States and the Soviet Union, the most populous in Communist China, and the economic super power in Japan. About half of the population of the world live in the states whose shorelines are washed by the Pacific Ocean.

Geography also lays the firm foundation of the Soviet Union's claim to be an Asian power. Two-thirds of Soviet territory lie to the East of the Urals, and extend due east to the Pacific coast, and border with traditional maritime powers of Asia such as Korea and Japan. To the South-East a further 4,000 miles of frontier is shared with the great power of Asia, Communist China, traditionally an uneasy neighbour. The Soviet territories in the Far East are vast empty tracts of land rich in raw materials, but totally empty of indigenous populations. Thus with very few exceptions the settlements in the Soviet Pacific provinces are European transplants peopled by European settlers. Cities such as Vladivostok and Khabarousk are European cities not Asian, and they are indicative of the accidental approach of the Soviet Union to the Pacific region. It is important to appreciate that although the Russians have followed a policy of expansion and territorial extension, which since the eighteenth century has given them an Asian presence, they represent the interests of a European state in an alien environment. In this sense the Soviet presence in Vladivostok, at least in geo-political terms, is as much a foreign intrusion in indigenous Asian eyes as that of the British in Hong Kong, or the Americans in Subic Bay.

As we have seen the Pacific in maritime affairs represents for the Russians the scene of their public humiliation at the hands of the Japanese in 1903.[3] In more recent times the Soviet Pacific Fleet provided the nucleus for their modern navy for it was the only naval force to survive the ravages of the Second World War intact. Its cruisers and destroyers waged a week of warfare on Japan and made possible the speedy occupation of the Kuril islands and the northern part of the Korean peninsula. The close of World War II, however, left the United States indisputably the master of the entire Pacific and its navy there, the greatest in the world, could see in that wide ocean no rival to oppose it; in contrast Soviet 'Pacific Adventures' seemed quite puny. The Korean War underlined the fact that the unchallenged naval power of the United States gave it complete access to any littoral state in the Pacific in which it might choose to intervene.

Thus subdued it was not until 1959 that the Soviet Pacific Fleet began to move out of the confines of its bases into the open seas. In that year a *Sverdlov* class cruiser, accompanied by two destroyers visited Djakarta and thus opened a new maritime link between the Soviet Union and Indonesia. Over the next four years Indonesia was supplied with a complete 'off the shelf' navy[4] including a *Sverdlov* class cruiser, eight destroyers, eight frigates, a dozen *Whisky* class submarines and a host of missile torpedo and gun boats. This link with the Soviet Union ended with the abrupt and dramatic fall from power of Sukarno in 1965. By this time the United States, having developed the longer ranged Polaris A3 missile had deployed a tender to Guam in support of submarine patrols in the Far East. As in other waters the Soviet navy responded with a forward deployment and an increased emphasis on anti-submarine warfare capabilities.

The Pacific contribution to the 1970 *Exercise Okean* saw a deployment of a squadron led by a *Sverdlov* class cruiser into the Philippine Sea. However, the most open and blatant demonstration of Soviet seapower was in the autumn of 1971, when a task force led by a *Kresta* class cruiser and comprising two *Kashin* class destroyers, a cruise-missile submarine, two diesel-powered attack submarines and a support ship, sailed deep into the Pacific through the Hawaian. Islands and in sight of the American naval complex on Oahu Island.

The Soviet Pacific Fleet operates out of two main bases, the traditional base at Vladivostock close to the Korean frontier and Petro-Pavlovsk which is located 1,000 miles to the North-East on the barren and inhospitable Kamchatka peninsula.[5] The fleet which is estimated to deploy more than one hundred submarines (of which about forty are nuclear) and sixty major surface combat ships now sees its main task as countering Communist Chinese activities.[6] Originally the fleet was intended to balance the American threat, but the schism with Peking, coupled to a withdrawal of the United States from Indo-China, has placed a different order in their list of strategic priorities.

The United States Navy maintains two distinct fleets in the Pacific. The Third Fleet operates in the Eastern Pacific and with its six carriers is responsible for the security of the United States west coast and the long-sea route to Honolulu. The Seventh Fleet, now reduced to two carriers and operating out of Subic Bay in the Philippines, and with additional facilities available in Taiwan, Japan, and South Korea, projects American naval power in the Western Pacific and Asian waters. The Island of Oahu and Pearl Harbour have remained the pivoting centre for the largest combined command in the world. The Commander-in-Chief Pacific is a four star Admiral and there are another fifty-one officers of flag-rank in the huge headquarters. The zone of responsibility for the Pacific Command stretches from the Persian Gulf to San Francisco. It is 2,000 miles from the Golden Gate to the first landfall at Hawaii, and from Oahu to the Polaris base at Apra Bay in Guam is a further 3,500 miles and therefore it is further from Hawaii to Guam than it is from Hawaii to New York. The Central and Western Pacific is a vast region, distances are enormous and land in consequence is at a premium. The military value of island territories can be seen in the stationing of strategic weapons in a forward deployment, the staging and support of conventional forces, and as bases from which to mount surveillance operations. Island territories are ideal for the deployment of nuclear submarines, because forward-basing increases their effectiveness by eliminating transit time. However, many Pacific islands while possessing good harbours, are not extensive enough to provide modern airstrips and runways, from which long-range strategic freighters can maintain the necessary air links. There are very few Pacific atolls which can provide the long runways for the modern airforce and a deep water harbour; Guam in the Marianas is one of the very few that can meet all these needs.

In the Asian Pacific waters the United States Navy has increasingly over the last few years found itself in a new and rather strange role of observing and even balancing the rival naval power of the Soviet Union and mainland China. Since the severing of the Russian connection, the naval arm of the Peoples' Liberation Army has been extensively modernized and has by all reliable accounts tripled in size. In terms of submarines, naval aviation and personnel, it is the third largest navy in the world. It has a total fleet strength of over 1,000 ships manned by 230,000 seamen and supported by a reserve of a million men with 5,000 additional vessels. Despite this size[7] the emphasis is on inshore coastal defence and control of territorial waters. The Navy is organized into three main fleets with about half the total strength concentrated with the 'East Sea Fleet' at Shanghai and Chou San Island. The 'North Sea Fleet' is based at Tsingatao and Lu Shun (Port Arthur), while the 'South Sea Fleet' is centred at Huang-Pa near Canton and Chan Chiang opposite Hainan Island.

The Soviet Navy which clearly sees this force as a threat would have to confront a powerful, well-armed and equipped naval power in China. The destroyers, escorts and frigates are a mixture of old Soviet vessels, Chinese copies and a few new vessels of indigenous design.[8] There is in addition a heavy emphasis on surface-to-surface missiles in the Chinese Navy. The naval doctrine expounded by Peking seems to be that which the Russians from their own recent past should understand, the concept of Sea Denial. The core of Chinese defence is the vast fleet of more than 700 missile, torpedo and gun-boats which would operate in conjunction with the coastal submarines and under the air umbrella of naval aviation.

Despite super power détente, the US withdrawal from Indo-China and the improvement in Sino-American relations, the regions of Pacific Asia still contain the ingredients and potential for conflict, both between the local indigenous states and at a limited level involving a super power. From Subic Bay in the South through Taiwan, the Ryukyu islands, to the Northern tip of Japan, the United States hems in the Communist powers along almost 2,000 miles of island bases and client states. Amongst the littoral states and those who live in the Pacific, there is no significant naval power outside the super powers, though some of the smaller powers such as South Korea, Japan, and Indonesia are able to deploy sufficient strength to restrict movement through strategically vital and narrow channels. In a region of shallow water tailor-made for mine warfare, and where such a strategem proved successful at Haiphong, all these powers have the capability to follow the American precedent. I believe that in the long run the United States may well come to regret its demonstration of such a potent and economy-crippling device as the mining of harbour entrances.

Outside the super power confrontations the conflict scenario within this region breaks down into two broad categories. In the first instance these remain the on-going areas of tension and possible conflict, such as the Korea peninsula. The unstable and irredentist North Koreans have on a number of occasions humiliated the United States[9] but nevertheless are held in check by the presence of the Seventh Fleet and the American presence in the Republic of South Korea. The South Korean Navy is strong and the Army is modern and well-trained, supported by a combat-ready US division.[10] The super powers seek to restrain their respective clients and maintain a balance of power[11] but it is a fragile structure and the potential for rupture must be very real.

About the only question upon which the Russians and the Chinese share any affiliation is their fear of Japan. The resurgence of Japanese naval might is constrained by many things, the not least of which is Article IX of the Constitution,[12] but the two mainland powers show considerable unease at the quality and efficiency of the Maritime Self Defence Force. Japan with a population of 108 millions packed into a territory the size of California is almost totally devoid of natural—especially energy—resources. For Japan is the world's leading shipbuilding nation, second in shipping and fishing, is a ravenous consumer of raw materials and has still to recover from the oil shock of the Middle East embargo of 1973. This made the Japanese all the more aware in the first instance of their jugular life-line to the Persian Gulf, and a recent Government report forecast oil consumption by 1985 to be in the region of 600 million tons. This horrific figure, which is equal to the total output of the Middle East in 1974, would require one 200,000 ton super tanker every twenty-five miles between Japan and the Gulf. Statistics such as these have caused the Japanese to discuss even more openly the extension of their maritime forces which alarms the Russians[13] and the Chinese. Russo-Japanese relations are in any case strained over the vexed question of the Soviet occupation of the Kuril Islands, while the Chinese resent the Japanese possession of the Senkaku Islands.[14]

Attention on these islands by the local powers points to the other likely cause of tension and possible conflict, coastal exploration and exploitation of energy resources. The shallow floor of the Continental Shelf off the coast of China extends for more than 2,000 miles from the Yellow Sea southwards through the East and South China Seas. Demands for oil have increased annually by as much as 40 per cent in both Taiwan and South Korea, and these coastal waters geologically promise to be an oil bonanza. The problem is that none of the states, whether friend or foe, are prepared to await the outcome of political agreements and there is unlikely to be a repeat of the 'gentlemanly' subdivision of the North Sea. Japan, with 1,500 miles of coastline, is a frightened nation and has already known the ravages of maritime blockade, and is anxious to undertake major off-shore operations. The Japanese recognize the median principle while both Taiwan and mainland China operate according to the principle of natural prolongation of land territory. The Republic of Korea seems to fall somewhere between the two and thus the scene is set for a type of 'wildcat competition' with each state making some vague assertions that it operates according to international law.

Islands such as Senkaku, Spratly and Paracel now assume an importance far in excess of their size. No territorial dispute between the countries of Eastern Asia has ever been resolved by international law and diplomacy, a factor which was underlined in 1974 when Communist China ousted the South Vietnamese from the Paracels.

It is against this background of new quarrels and traditional rivalries that one must observe and measure the deployment of the Soviet Pacific Fleet, the US Seventh Fleet and the developing naval power of Communist China. Each of them has its problems. For the United States a continued forward projection and dual capability of a carrier presence in both the Pacific and Indian Oceans will depend as much on diplomatic relations with the Philippines,[15] the integrity of access routes through the Indonesian Archipelago, as much as on budgetry restraints at home or the will of the American Congress. The Soviet Union continues diplomatically to seek to contain China, and to re-adjust the Asian alignments in such a manner that Moscow will no longer be the odd man out in the East Asian Quadrilateral of Powers. To this end the Russians will seek to improve relations with Tokyo without losing control of the strategically important Kuril Islands. At present the Soviet Government believes that with the death of Chairman Mao the Chinese leadership will become even more radical and extremist.[16] Soviet experts foresee a return to the old tempestuous days of the Sino-Soviet dispute and thus prepare their forces for an uncertain future in the Far East. At the same time the Russians continue to win favour with Hanoi and seek to oust Chinese influence elsewhere in Indo-China.

The Chinese, for their part, are rumoured to be moving rapidly towards the construction of a submarine-launched missile system. This would be an obvious direction for them to pursue and with the *Han* class submarine which is reported to be nuclear-powered and their one *Golf* class[17] they presumably have the test beds for such a project. In a rather perverse manner both of the mainland Communist powers recognize in the American presence an important element in their security. The Chinese use the American Navy as a shield behind which they build their own, and Peking does not wish to see the demise of the United States as an Asian Power. Taiwan is a complicating factor in Sino-American relations, and Peking, given the right political conditions, probably now disposes sufficient military power to launch an invasion of the Nationalist redoubt. However, such is the strategic importance of the position of Taiwan that both Peking and Moscow would prefer the islands' configuration to remain than for either to see the other in possession.

Notes

1. June 1942 four Japanese carriers were sunk and the spearhead of Japanese aviation irrevocably damaged.
2. There are only three deep-water channels: Sanda, Lombok and Witar.
3. See Chapter One.

4. Indonesia obtained 104 ships from the USSR, though all are now apparently stricken from the active list.

5. It has the advantage of facing open sea, unlike Vladivostock which is enclosed by the Sea of Japan, although the isolation of Petropavlovsk makes it vulnerable to a surgical strike in a limited nuclear exchange. Nevertheless the bulk of the Soviet *Yankee* class SLBMS which are deployed with the Pacific Fleet operate out of the Petropavlovsk base.

6. This task applies to the surface units. The SLBMs cruise off the western coast of the USA and, in any case, the waters around the Chinese coast are not suitable for SLBMS.

7. Even then these figures do not take into account the countless junks which could be pressed into service.

8. Particularly impressive are the seventy Hu Chuan hydrofoil torpedo boats which have been under construction since the late fifties. The Red Navy includes a new class of 3,750 ton destroyers.

9. The Pueblo Incident in particular but on a couple of occasions the North Koreans have downed US Maritime reconnaissance aircraft over the Sea of Japan.

10. There is one US Army division with the same alert status as US Seventh Army in Germany and performing a similar trip-wire function.

11. The North Koreans have a strong airforce but its navy has only a limited amphibious capability while the South Korean Navy has a strong amphibious force but its own airforce would need American support in any major operations. On 6 October 1975 a North Korean intelligence vessel was sunk by South Korean Airforce.

12. Article IX of the Constitution prescribes the maintenance of land, sea and air forces as well as other potential for war-making.

13. The 1972 Revision of the Ryukyu chain has extended the Japanese coastline and expanded the concept of maritime home defence to more than 1,000 miles out from the Home Islands.

14. Returned to Japan by the United States in 1972. The Japanese claim is a thin one and is seriously challenged by the Chinese who, by all accounts, have a strong legal case. The five islands in the chain are situated some 200 miles west of Okinawa, they are uninhabited and the biggest is barely two miles long. For a long while these islands have been used only as a navigation reference but the prospect of oil in the region raises their importance enormously.

15. President Marcos of the Philippines visited Peking in June 1975 and formal diplomatic relations were established. This was followed by a fair degree of agitation against the extensive American base in Subic Bay and elsewhere. However, recently the neutralist cries have been quietened by 30,000 Filipinos who are employed directly by the American forces and represent a facet of the Philippine economy which is ignored at Manila's peril.

16. Moscow apparently expects those radicals grouped around Chairman Mao's wife Chiang Ching to be near the centre of power when the 'Great Helmsman' died.

17. *Golf* Ballistic Missile type with the tubes fitted into the conning tower.

CHAPTER ELEVEN

Conclusions. The Soviet Navy: Myth and Reality

On the 18th July 1975 the *Kiev*, Russia's brand-new 40,000 ton aircraft carrier and pride of the fleet passed under the Bosphorus Bridge and through the Dardanelles, en route to the Northern Fleet, for its first operational cruise. The *Kiev* which is a symbol of sea-power in the classical sense, sailed via the Aegean, which in turn symbolises the nature of maritime conflict in the contemporary world. The contrast is both immediate and disturbing for the Aegean threatens to erupt as the focus of a conflict between Greece and Turkey over exploitation of the seabed, and is a part of the world where the Soviet Union as the newly-arrived global maritime power has a vested interest in unrestricted passage and freedom of navigation on the high seas.

The arrival of the *Kiev* makes complete the claim of the Soviet Union to be a global maritime power and fulfills the hopes and aspirations entertained by Stalin[1] in the years immediately before the Second World War. But what sort of role is this aircraft carrier, together with its attendant escorts, going to fulfil at sea in the eighties? The whole concept of modern seapower revolves around the vexed question of the aircraft carrier at sea in the future. On the one hand both the British and Americans are maintaining their investment in naval airpower but have come up with different answers: the British developing *The Invincible*[2] while the Americans still laying out vast sums on super carriers on the lines of the *Nimitz*.[3] Politicians and statesmen on both sides of the Atlantic are beginning to question the wisdom of these policies and, not for the first time, question whether navies are preparing for a war they will never have to fight. The aircraft carrier is at the centre of this controversy for to the professional seaman it is indicative of the power and status of the nation, while to the layman it is becoming the symbol of doubt and frustration with the increasingly chairborne admirals. It is reasonable to assume that this debate is not the exclusive province of the Western world but that the Politburo questions the role of the Soviet Navy. Gorshkov after years of endeavour has now succeeded in destroying the concept of American naval hegemony, but he has not been able to replace it with the Red Fleet. So how does the Soviet leadership feel about their seapower? and what role do they see it performing in the future? Will they, and dare they use it as an extension and physical symbol of power, as the Victorians used the nineteenth-century Royal Navy? or will they, as continentalists, be reluctant to give it free rein on the high seas? Can a leadership which is doctrinaire, riddled with theory, and hitherto stereotyped in its thinking, adopt a brand-new approach to a maritime extension of Soviet Foreign Policy? These are questions for which only time can provide an answer.

I have attempted to illustrate in this book how the Soviet Navy has emerged, especially since the days of questionable performance during the Second World War, into an impressive and modern navy displaying an array of maritime talent and expertise which, with the *Kiev*, is now complete. Of course, the objectives and the policy purposes which have moulded the shape, structure and mission of the Soviet Fleet must remain largely a closed book. All the evidence available, other than assessment of ships, is centred around the now prolific writings of Admiral Gorshkov.[4] The prime mission of the Soviet Navy, which is shared by the navies of the United States, Great Britain, France and, presumably in the near future, Communist China, is that of strategic deterrence provided by the fleet of ballistic missile-armed submarines. Some commentators liken the Polaris-type submarine to the capital ship of the modern navy, but I find this very misleading. These ships do not compare with the battleships or even aircraft carriers of the past as the physical symbols of national pride and prestige. Neither in the military sense do they qualify, for they are not the mighty instruments around which the rest of the fleet gather for protection. In a very real way the strategic submarines in the jigsaw equations of nuclear deterrence do not belong in any discussion of seapower. However, to exclude such vessels is to over-simplify the discussion, for the means of their counter-other nuclear submarines, maritime air, and destroyers in the ASW role—is at the heart of the complex issue of seapower.

The impressive surface units of the Soviet Navy seek, in the first instance, to support the missions of the strategic submarines by sweeping the seas clear of Western anti-submarine forces and denying, in a *surge deployment,* the West access to vital waterways. In time of peace these ships will continue to be used by the navy, though in a slightly reduced form, to further Russian interests by asserting a presence in those parts of the world which the Soviet Government consider to be of importance. The United States and the Soviet Union are the two dominant naval powers on the contemporary world scene for together they share a common interest in the global expression of that seapower through unimpeded access to the high seas. It is this commonality of power which draws the United States and the Soviet Union together, and produces the same sort of problems in their dealings with other and smaller states. To a degree the relative freedom that both of these states can enjoy on the high seas will be conditioned by the restraints that mutually govern the rules of their own competition and rivalry.[5] Their surveillance either by aircraft or satellite, shadowing above and below the waves, could increasingly be controlled by procedures agreed in Arms Control Conferences.[6] However, freedom of navigation will also be conditional on the attitudes, desires and policies of smaller coastal states, and these, allies apart, will be influenced by economic and political considerations, as much as the military factor.

The writings of Alfred Thayer Mahan could not have been concerned with the role of navies as instruments of strategic delivery but neither was he aware of what many would now see increasingly as the role of seapower in the last quarter of the twentieth century, that of national defender of seabed resources. Over the last few years the United Nations has sought to achieve international consensus on seabed resources, the sea, and coastal boundaries. Individual nations continue to differ over what should constitute an Exclusive Economic Zone (EEZ), but such is the cumbersome nature of the political process, that states are increasingly less willing to delay exploration and exploitation in the hope that international consensus can be reached. Small coastal states, wracked by inflation and heavily dependent upon the political health of others for their vital needs, are desperate to develop what they see as rightly their's on the doorstep of their shoreline. Unilateral declarations of 200-mile territorial limits and EEZ's of conflicting proportions will shortly herald the start of the last great enclosure movement in history, the enclosure of the seabed. The creation of these economic zones will bring some thirty-five per cent of the oceans under the control of states, an area equal to the total landmass of the earth. How such a move will effect issues such as freedom of navigation is hard to predict, though in the last resort it will rest on bilateral agreements between the resident power and those who seek transit or access. In what remains of the high seas the traditional freedom to navigate, to fish, and to undertake a host of other activities will be increasingly subject to challenge.

As the search for natural resources[7] expands into a major off-shore occupation, states are bound to become jealous of their sovereignty in what they regard as territorial waters. This does not necessarily mean that a major naval power will feel inhibited or constrained in the movement of its warships, but such deployments might well be achieved only at the cost of insulting a state sensitive over the violation of its maritime frontier. It does seem that the Soviet Union has emerged as the last great defender of the freedom of the seas, and has arrived with a 'blue water capability' just when this ancient instrument of statecraft could be losing some of its instrumentality.

Another factor which is particularly apt in this context is that whereas in the past the small coastal state had to sit back in anguished impotence while its territorial waters were violated by the so-called big navies, this in the future need no longer be the case. In the first instance the small state can mobilize immediate and ready-made majorities in organizations such as the General Assembly of the United Nations, where the stalking of great powers through motions of censure has become almost a way of life. Secondly small navies now possess the means to deny the big neighbour the capability of acting with impunity. If seapower is being revolutionized by the enclosure of the seabed, then sea warfare has been revolutionized by the development of the anti-ship missile. The missile-armed gunboat does present a really substantial threat to the big ship navies. Firstly such weapon systems though they are very sophisticated can be 'purchased' in a suitcase pack whereby they require little more than a simple installation and the willpower to press the button. Missiles like the Soviet 'Styx', the Norwegian 'Penguin' and the Israeli 'Gabriel' are self-contained weapons whose very sophistication allows the unsophisticated to operate them. Thus by the simple expedient of taking the advanced technology out of the ship and placing it into the weapon (it comes in a sealed pack which is literally plugged-in) missiles are brought into the operational capabilities of small navies. The main advantage of the missile over the gun is that it provides enormous and guaranteed killing power for a light weight to the extent that the missile can equalize the hitting power of ships of unequal size. Defence against missiles has absorbed the energies and budgets of the major naval powers at an ever-increasing rate over the last decade. The options are first to destroy the missile itself, either with an anti-missile, with gunfire,[8] or with electronic counter-measures. But the only problem is that such installations are expensive, space-consuming and with a missile travelling at transonic speed or more leaves little margin for error, and no second chance. The alternative is to take out the missile platform in the shape of a fast moving gunboat at a range of some forty miles. Until quite recently the missile boats presented a threat from beyond the main gun armament of most Western warships.[9] Thus ships could only be defended by indigenous air support whether helicopters, conventional or Vstol aircraft, armed with air-to-surface missiles. It would be quite wrong to assume that weak coastal states would necessarily feel any more inhibitions, or indeed the same constraints, about attacking the ships of a great power than the great powers feel towards one another. Decisive action could well be the prerogative of the weak against the strong especially as contemporary politics reveal the tendency of small states to increasingly disregard the rules of the game as followed by the established powers. Small states can act irresponsibly and more than ever are prepared to play the game of international diplomacy by their own rules.

Clearly seapower, as an instrument of diplomacy, is more heavily constrained than ever before and it is in this new international environment that one has to assess Soviet maritime intentions and capabilities. This, however, does not deny seapower a traditional utility as an extension of government to the manner which was understood and propagated by Mahan. Seapower, whether it is intended for control of the sea or the projection of power ashore, has a number of characteristics which have an advantage over other forms of military power. There is a universality about seapower for the seas are an international medium which allow for the projection of naval force into distant territories. Secondly, seapower is a highly flexible instrument of statecraft and differing emphasis and interpretations can be conveyed by variations in size and activity. Finally, it seems appropriate, especially in the context of the Soviet Navy, to emphasise the 'visibility' of sea power. By being observed on the high seas, in foreign ports, or off alien coasts, a naval presence can convey a warning or a threat to a disruptive state and provide stability and succour to a troubled client. These forms of naval power, or 'naval suasion', have been practised by the United States since the Second World War and by Britain for even longer, but the advent of the Soviet Navy has produced a situation in which resorts to 'naval suasion' by either side are conditional in a way that has never been before. In any case the ability of either super power to use its navies in pursuit of diplomatic objectives is bound to be limited because of the over-whelming need to neutralize one another.[10] In a self-cancelling process this degree of shipping available for other purposes will be limited, probably obsolescent, and seen as a secondary role.

How strong is the Soviet Navy? This, as I have attempted to show, is an almost impossible question to answer today because the index of maritime strength is not measured in terms of the numbers of aircraft carriers, cruisers or submarines that a particular power deploys. The big navies of the past always prepared for the same objective, the decisive sea battle, be that a Trafalgar, Jutland or Midway. By the same token there are those who would draw historical parallels between the navies of the super powers today and the naval race[11] between Britain and Imperial Germany in the years before the Great War. I find the parallel quaint, especially when taken with a comparison of Gorshkov with Tirpitz, but misleading since it sees seapower from this classical orthodox viewpoint. The new systems of naval power which we have examined are not as obvious nor spectacular as symbols of nationhood and national prestige. Instead the complex naval systems deployed by the super powers as indications of the political values of their state are quite incalculable.

So what of the future? The Soviet Union despite the deployment of the *Kiev* has in recent years actually reduced the numbers of active units in the Fleet. Whether this is due to phased obsolescence with a replacement programme running behind schedule, a new shift in economic and budgetary priorities, or whether this is a qualitative trend which aims to produce fewer but better ships is difficult to tell. The United States shows all the signs of continuing to interpret maritime balance as an overwhelming superiority and, with an emotional entanglement and attachment to the aircraft carrier, will continue to invest vast fortunes in these steel goliaths that have little relevance to the needs of modern seapower. Despite the continued dedication of Congress to the tenets of a Blue Water Navy it seems to me that the days of the United States regarding the Pacific Ocean as an American lake are limited. However, all the trends point to the naval arm of the People's Liberation Army bringing this to a close rather than the Soviet Pacific Fleet based at Vladivostock.

In the Indian Ocean the development of American facilities in areas such as Diego Garcia will in the short-term simply prompt the Soviet Union into seeking some form of permanent presence. However, in this region in particular it is the influence of the navies of the littoral states which will increasingly predominate. Given time, states such as India and Iran[12] will develop from coastal powers to a mid-ocean capability and perhaps will signal the end of the period which began with Vasco da Gama, namely wherever there is an ocean there is a European presence.

Naval technology and new developments in weapon systems will continue to exert their decisive influence over ship configurations and deployments. These are, by their very nature, discreet subjects and there is little to be said except to point out that should warfare occur at sea in the 1980s it will probably be as different to the conflicts of the mid-twentieth century as they were to those of the American Civil War. Although the naval missile has exerted such tremendous influence it seems now that navies are coming away from their love affair and returning to the gun as a complementary weapon. The Soviet Union, together with the United States, will continue to develop their submarine missile systems. Although these are very expensive weapon systems they are likely to remain largely invulnerable and as the potency and accuracy of the land-based ICBMS improves this trend to the sea will continue. But the seabed is an eerie arena for confrontation for it is difficult to identify a missile submarine from other submarines and other forms of acoustic interference such as fish and noise.

The theme that I have presented throughout this chapter is that the Soviet Union as a major naval power has a number of shared interests with the United States. In addition I have tried to present the Soviet Navy as an impressive, modern, well-equipped fighting force, but one that is constrained by a whole series of considerations in its expression of seapower, many of which are shared in common with other sea-going nations. I have made very little reference to Soviet mercantile capability and intentions because I do not see this as a sinister force bent upon the economic dislocation of the Western world. If my theme throughout is that the Soviet Union has a stake in the maritime affairs of the world and has largely abided by the rules of the game, then this also applies to the mercantile marine. The merchant fleet which has undergone a programme of considerable expansion since the mid-fifties, has done so largely for economic reasons. It is true that very little Soviet trade needs to go by sea, but the Soviet Union does need to earn hard currencies to pay for Western imports. It is clear that the mercantile marine was expanded essentially as a means of improving the Soviet balance of payments and any military or political advantages were purely ancilliary. The figures for the fishing fleet distort the Soviet mercantile tonnage in terms of the world league and a completely different picture is produced when ships below a 1,000 tons are excluded.[13] The Soviet Union has attempted on a number of occassions to undercut internationally agreed carriage rates but such is the sophistication of the system that they have invariably come to heel and abided by the rules of competition. The competitive nature of the Soviet mercantile marine is enhanced by the fact that it is state-owned and the profit motive is less important. However, this advantage is balanced by the uncompetitive capability of the Soviet Fleet in the twin directions of modern merchant marines, containerisation and bulk carriers.

Conflict at sea caused by the sea is clearly on the agenda of international relations in the final quarter of the century. Some commentators go further and less realistically envisage that conflict being a limited war between the super powers limited geographically to the sea and in weapons to those beneath the nuclear threshold. The former presents a myriad of possibilities involving quarrels over resources and frontiers, pollution and passage, in which the super power navies with their interests clearly bound in freedom of passage and access, could well find the convergence of interests which I have already discussed. Whether this intriguing possibility is a viable one only time will tell, but conflict at sea, of the type I have discussed, will set the context for the employment of the navies of the super power. It is against this background as much as a comparison with the United States that the intentions and capabilities of the Soviet Navy have to be measured. By all the measures of comparison available to us at present, there is no evidence to suggest that the Soviet Union is spending any more than is necessary on their navy to ensure the security of the state.[14]

Finally in relation to the tasks outlined by Gorshkov one cannot avoid the conclusion that the Soviet Navy is already over-extended. Throughout its post-war history the Red Fleet has been a reaction to an American and Western seapower and I do not envisage any reversal of this trend.

Notes

1. See Chapter II.
2. HMS *Invincible*
3. USS *Nimitz*.
4. See p. 70, note 1.
5. 1972 Soviet American Incidents at Sea Treaty.
6. The Americans have proposed on a number of occasions at Arms Control Conferences the creation and mutual recognition of patrol sanctuaries for SLBMs.
7. And in this category one would include fish as well as oil and natural gas.
8. Navies have developed all these forms of counter:
   (a) The Americans have developed *Aegis* which is a shipborne area defence system against anti-ship cruise missiles: CIWS (close in weapon system) which is a standard six barrel Vulcan cannon firing 3,000 rounds of 20 mm shells per minute.
   (b) The Russian equivalent of CIWS are pairs of small mountings of automatic cannon.
   (c) Most air defence missiles have an anti-missile capability and so do the latest rapid fire gun armaments.
9. The basic DP single 5 inch 54 calibre Mark 42 Mounting which has equipped most American warships in the recent past has a maximum range of 13 nautical miles. The new American 8 inch (203 mm) MCLWG Major Calibre Light Weight Gun which will equip the Spruance class destroyers is intended primarily for shore bombardment. The main defence will still be anti-ship cruise missiles of the 'Exocet' and 'Harpoon' variety.
10. For example the movement of American carriers into the Indian Ocean did produce a Soviet response which in turn has resulted in an 'expensive post operative care operation' by the USA in terms of surveillance and shadowing of subsequent Soviet activity.
11. If there is a 'naval race' then the Americans are 'winning'. Congressional Hearings in February 1976 were informed by Admiral James Holloway that in the fifteen years to 1975 the United States had built 122 surface warships of 3,000 tons or more, while the Soviet Union built only 57. New York Times Service, March 1976.
12. The new fleet it is rumoured will be built around an *Invincible* class purchased from Britain and the *Spruance* class of destroyers from the United States.

13. Figures quoted for 1971 and published by the US Department of Commerce; Maritime Administration, Merchant Fleets of the World, ocean-going steam and motorships of 1,000 gross tons and over, show the Soviet Union to be the sixth in the batting league, with Liberia, Japan, Great Britain, Norway and Greece ahead. For a fuller account of Soviet mercantile activity see the article by Robert E. Athay in Chapter 7 *Soviet Naval Developments Capability and Context*, ed. Michael McGuire: Praeger, 1973.

14. Thus only ten per cent of the Soviet Defence Budget is allocated to the navy while the United States spends thirty per cent.

Soviet Naval Strengths/Deployments[1]

CLASS	NORTH	BALTIC	BLACK SEA*	PACIFIC	TOTAL
SUBMARINES					
DELTA II	1	—	—	—	1
DELTA	5	—	—	—	5
YANKEE	25	—	—	8	33
HOTEL III	1	—	—	—	1
HOTEL II	5	—	—	3	8
CHARLIE	11	—	—	—	11
ECHO II	15	—	—	12	27
ECHO I	—	—	—	1	1
VICTOR	12	—	—	2	14
NOVEMBER	9	—	—	5	14
GOLF I & II	14	—	—	8	22
ZULU V	1	—	—	—	1
JULIET	11	—	—	5	16
WHISKY TWIN CYLINDER	—	—	—	—	5
WHISKY LONG BIN	5	2	1	4	7
ALPHA	1	—	—	—	1
BRAVO	1	1	1	1	4
TANGO	1	—	—	—	1
FOXTROT	31	14	—	11	56
ROMEO	—	5	9	—	14
QUEBEC	—	11	11	—	22
ZULU	9	4	—	4	17
WHISKY	20	40	22	28	110
WHISKY CANVAS BAG	1	—	—	2	3
TOTAL ON STATION	179	77	44	94	394
ASW CARRIER					
KURIL	—	—	1 + 1	—	1 + 1
CRUISERS					
KARA	—	—	2	—	2
MOSKVA	—	—	2	—	2
SVERDLOV	2	3	4	3	12
CHAPAEV	1	1	—	—	2
KIROV	—	1	1	—	2
KRESTA II	3	2	2	—	6
KRESTA I	3	—	—	1	4
KYNDA	—	—	2	2	4
TOTAL ON STATION	9	7	14	6	36

[1]Data taken from 'Janes' 1975 edition.
*Includes Caspian

CLASS	NORTH	BALTIC	BLACK SEA*	PACIFIC	TOTAL
DESTROYER/TYPE					
KRIVAK	4	3	—	—	7
KASHIN	3	3	8	5	19
KANIN	3	2	—	1	6
KRUPNY	—	—	—	2	2
SAM KOTLIN	2	1	3	2	8
KILDIN	—	1	2	—	3
KOTLIN	3	3	4	8	19
TALLIN	—	1	—	—	1
SKORY	10	10	10	10	40
TOTAL ON STATION	25	24	27	28	104
FRIGATE/ESCORT ASD					
NANUCHKA	—	5	4	—	9
PETYA II	10	12	13	10	45
RIGA	10	9	12	9	40
GRISHA	3	5	4	2	14
KRONSTADT	7	4	4	5	20
POTI	25	26	5	15	70
MIRKA I + II	4	4	8	4	20
KOLA	—	1	3	2	6
SO I	—	40	30	10	80
TOTAL ON STATION	59	105	83	57	304
FLEET SWEEPERS	40	40	58	50	188
COASTAL SWEEPERS	27	45	25	25	123
LIGHT FORCES					
PCHELA (HYDROFOILS)	—	10	15	—	25
KOMAR	—	5	10	—	15
OSA	25	35	25	35	120
FAC. TORPEDO	15	70	20	45	150
TOTAL ON STATION	40	120	70	80	310
DEPOT/SUPPORT SHIPS					
UGRA	4	2	—	2	8
LAMA	2	—	1	2	5
DON	3	—	—	3	6
ASSAULT SHIPS	14	19	21	18	72
LANDING CRAFT	10	15	30	20	75
INTELLIGENCE SHIPS (AGIs)	15	8	15	15	53

*Includes Caspian.

Soviet Naval Missiles

Type	System Nato Code	Ship	Range (n/miles)	Tube Launches	Comments
A) STRATEGIC MISSILES (SLBMS)					
STRATEGIC	SS-N-8 —	5+14 'DELTA' SUBMARINE	4,200	12	Operational in 1973/Poseidon
STRATEGIC	SS-M-6 SAWFLY	33 'YANKEE' SUBMARINE	1,300	16	Operational in 1969/Polaris A3
STRATEGIC	SS-M-5 SERB	11 GOLF II SUBMARINE 8 HOTEL II SUBMARINE 1 ZULU V SUBMARINE	700	3 3 2	Operational in 1963
STRATEGIC	SS-M-4 SARK	11 GOLF I SUBMARINE	300	3	Operational in 1958 now being phased out
B) ANTI-SHIP CRUISE MISSILES (SSM CRUISE)					
SSM (CRUISE)	SS-M-1 SCRUBBER	2 'KILDIN' DESTROYERS 2 'KRUPNY' DESTROYERS	130	1 2	Subsonic and obsolescent
SSM (CRUISE)	SS-N-2 STYX	15 'KOMAR' FAC 65 'OSA' I FAC	23	2 4	Operational since 1960. Western missiles: Grocer, Penguin Gabriel

TYPE	SYSTEM NATO CODE	SHIP	RANGE (n/miles)	TUBE LAUNCHES	COMMENTS
SSM (Cruise)	SS-N-3	SHADDOCK			
		4 'Kynda' Cruisers		8	Operational since 1962.
		4 'Kresta' I Cruisers		4	Needs over longer radar direction source
		16 'Juliet' Submarines		4	
		1 'Echo' I Submarines		6	
		27 'Echo' II Submarines	150/250	8	
		7 'Whisky Long Bin' Submarines		4	
		5 'Whisky Twin Cylinder' Submarines		2	
	SS-N-7	11 'Charlie' Submarines	30	8	Subsurface launch operational 1970. Harpoon eventually as a Western weapon.

C) ANTI-SHIP MISSILES (SSM)

TYPE	SYSTEM NATO CODE	SHIP	RANGE (n/miles)	TUBE LAUNCHES	COMMENTS
SSM	SS-N-9	1 'Delta II' Submarine	150	16	Operational in 1969
SSM	SS-N-10	9 'Nanuchka' Missile Corvettes		6	Operation in 1968. Exocet etc. as a Western weapon.
		2 'Kara' Cruisers		8	
		6 'Kresta II' Destroyers	29	8	
		7 'Krivak' Destroyers		4	
SSM	SS-N-11	55 'Osa II' FAC		4	Probably a modified Styx.
		1+2 Modified 'Kildin' Destroyer;	29	4	

D) *SURFACE TO AIR MISSILES (SAM)*

				(SLANT RANGE)	(ALL TWIN TUBES)	
SAM	SA-N-1	GOA	8 SAM KOTLIN DESTROYERS		1	Western equivalent as Sea Dart, Sea Slug.
			6 'KANIN' DESTROYERS		1	
			19 'KASHIN' DESTROYERS	17	2	
			4 'KYNDA' CRUISERS		1	
			4 'KRESTA I' CRUISERS		2	
SAM	SA-N-2	GUIDEZINE	1 'DZERZHINSKI' CRUISER	25	1	
SAM	SA-N-3	GOBLET	1+1 'KURIL' CARRIER		2	
			2 'MOSKVA' CRUISERS	20	2	
			6 'KRESTA II' CRUISERS		2	
SAM	SA-N-4	—	2 'KARA' CRUISERS		2	
			1+1 'KURIL' CARRIER		3	
			2 'SVERDLOV' CRUISERS	20	1	
			5 'KRIVAK' DESTROYERS		2	
			9 'NANUCHKA' CORVETTES		2	
			14 'GRISHA' CORVETTES		1	

E) *AIR TO SURFACE ANTI-SHIP MISSILES (ASM): FIGURES APPROXIMATE*

ASM	AS-1	KENNEL	50 BADGER 'B' BOMBER	55	2	Obsolete Transonic
ASM	AS-2	KIPPER	150 BADGER 'C' BOMBER	115	1	Obsolescent supersonic
ASM	AS-3	KANGAROO	20 BEAR B/C BOMBER	400	2	Mach 1.5
ASM	AS-4	KITCHEN	? BLINDER B BOMBER	185	1	Inertial guided
ASM	AS-5	KELT	150 BADGER G	120	2	
ASM	AS-6	—	50 BADGER 'MODIFIED'	300	2	Operational 1970

Initials	Meaning	Soviet Navy Class	Western Counterpart
SSBN	Ballistic Missile Submarines	Delta Yankee Hotel II	Trident U.S. Lafayette[1] U.K. Resolution
SSB	Ballistic Missile Submarines[2]	Golf II	None
SSGN	Cruise Missile Submarines Nuclear powered	Charlie/Echo II	None[3]
SSG	Cruise Missile Submarines with Shaddock Missiles	Juliet Whisky Long Bin	None
SSN	Fleet Submarines, nuclear powered torpedo armed	Victor November Uniform	USA Permit/Skipjack Los Angeles UK Valiant/Churchill Swiftshire
SS	Patrol submarines, conventionally powered	Tango Foxtrot Romeo Zulu IV Whisky V	USA Barber/Oberon Porpoise
CVAN/CVN	Nuclear powered attack carriers	Nil	Nimitz/Enterprise
CVA/CV	Attack Aircraft Carrier	Nil	Kitty Hawk/Forrestal Midway UK Ark Royal USA Hancock/Essex
CVS	Antisubmarine Carrier	Kuril	UK Hermes Invincible
CHG	Helicopter Cruisers	Moskva/Leningrad	USA Guam UK Tiger[4]

INITIALS	MEANING	SOVIET NAVY CLASS	WESTERN COUNTERPART
CGM CG	Nuclear powered guided missile cruiser Guided Missile Armed Cruisers	NIL KARA KRESTA II	USA LONG BEACH USA ALBANY UK NIL
CG	Guided Missile Armed Light Cruiser	KYNDA KRESTA I	USA CLEVELAND UK COUNTY/ BRISTOL
CLC	Gun armed conventional cruisers	SVERDLOV	USA }NIL UK }
DLGN	Nuclear powered guided missile frigates	NIL	USA VIRGINIA CALIFORNIA TRUXTUN BAINBRIDGE UK NIL
DDG	Guided missile frigates	KASHIN	USA COONTZ LEAHY BELKNAP UK SHEFFIELD
DDG	Guided Missile Destroyers	KANIN KRUPNY KRIVAK KOTLIN	USA FORREST SHERMAN CHARLES F. ADAMS UK NIL,
DD	Fleet Destroyers	KOTLIN SKORY TALIN	USA FORREST SHERMAN SPRUANCE GEARING UK NIL

INITIALS	MEANING	SOVIET NAVY CLASS	WESTERN COUNTERPART
FF	Frigates/Destroyer Escorts	RIGA PETYA II MIRKA II	USA NIL UK SALISBURY TYPE 14
PGG	Missile Armed Corvettes	NANOUCHLKA	USA NIL UK NIL
PCE	Patrol Corvettes	POTI KRONSTADT GRISHA	USA NIL UK NIL
AEM	Missile Support Ship (Repair)	LAMA	USA NIL UK NIL
AS	Submarine Support/Depot	UGRA/DON	USA VARIOUS SHIPS
AR	General Purpose Depot Ships	AMUR	UK MAIDSTONE USA VARIOUS SHIPS
LST	Amphibious Warfare Ship	ALLIGATOR	UK TRIUMPH USA NIL
FAC/M	Fast Attack Croft Missile	OSA/KOMAR	UK NIL USA NIL UK TENACITY

Notes:

1. The United States have confused the issue by classifying the *Lafayette* as FBMs Fleet Ballistic Missile Submarines. Throughout the list I have used this only with reference to the *Trident* class with its intercontinental range missile system. The full list of US Navy SSBNs by class is: *Trident*, *Lafayette*, *George Washington*, *Ethen Allen*.

2. These are the earlier version of Soviet SSBNs which were equipped with three launches for the *Sark* missile; after the conversion of the *Hotel* class they were converted to carry the 650 mile *Serb* missile and downgraded to 'second rate'.

3. Technically there are no Western equivalents to a Soviet submarine equipped with the subsurface launchers anti-ship cruise missile. Within a short while the United States will have produced the *Harpoon* missile (as the equivalent to the SS-N-7) and equip the later construction *Los Angeles* class of SSN.

4. The Cruiser *Invincible* is due to be completed in 1978. The Americans have designs for a helicopter cruiser which they describe as a 'Sea Control Ship'—the first is due to commission in 1978.

The Military Balance at Sea: The United States/ Soviet Union

Type/Class	Red Navy	USN
Fleet Ballistic Missile Submarines SSBN }	39	} 41
Attack Submarines — Nuclear (SSN)	66	} 59 + 27
Aircraft Carriers:		
Attack Carriers (CVAN)	—	1 + 3
(CVA)	—	13
Anti Submarine (CVS)	1	4
Cruisers:		
CAN	—	1
CG	8	3
CG	8	2
CLCP	14	—
Destroyers:		
DLGN	—	4 + 3
DDG	14	28
DDG	23	29
DD	72	70 + 23
Frigates/Escorts:		
DEG (Missile Escort Ships) FF	9	6
AGDE (Escort Ships)	125	60

Select Bibliography

BLECHMAN, Barry M. — *The Changing Soviet Navy* (The Brookings Institution, Washington D.C., 1973).

BREYER, Siegfried — *Guide to the Soviet Navy* (United States Naval Institute, Annapolis MD, 1970).

HERRICK, Robert Waring — *Soviet Naval Strategy* (United States Naval Institute, Annapolis MD, 1968).

HEWLETT, Richard G. and DUNCAN, Francis — *Nuclear Navy* (University of Chicago Press, Chicago and London, 1973).

KUENNE, Robert — *The Attack Submarine: A Study in Strategy* (Yale University Press, New Haven and London, 1965).

McGWIRE, Michael (ed.) — *Soviet Naval Development: Capability and Context* (Praeger, New York, 1973).

McGWIRE, Michael: (Ken Booth and John McDonnell, eds.) — *Soviet Naval Policy: Objectives and Constraints* (Praeger, New York, 1975).

PILMAR, Norman — *Soviet Naval Power: Challenge for the Seventies* (MacDonald & Janes, London, 1974).

THEBERGE, James (ed.) — *Soviet Seapower in the Caribbean: Political and Strategic Implications* (Praeger, New York, 1974).

For further reference:
Janes Fighting Ships 74/75. (Sampson and Low, London, 1974).
Janes Pocket Book of Major Warships Captain John Moore RN (ed.) (MacDonald & Janes, London, 1973).
United States Naval Institute Proceedings, Annapolis.
The Military Balance, London. The International Institute for Strategic Studies, 1974.

Index